Figures suggest that more than ten per cent of people in the workforce struggle with depression. Both employees and their managers are looking for the same outcome: recovery and return to best functioning. *Tackling Depression at Work* explains the key issues that arise and offers proven strategies that employees and managers can use. Topics of discussion include:

- the importance of education about depression and bipolar disorder
- how to support an employee without crossing boundaries
- the destigmatisation of mood disorders
- the sensitive issues of disclosure and privacy.

With insightful advice from workers who have learned to manage their disorder on the job, this book offers invaluable support for any worker with depression. It is also an essential resource for all line managers, human resource managers and mental health professionals.

Kerrie Eyers is a psychologist, teacher and editor with many years' of experience in mental health, based at the Black Dog Institute, Sydney, Australia.

Gordon Parker AO is Scientia Professor of Psychiatry at the University of New South Wales a
Dog Institute, Sydney, Australia
over 30 years' of experience wit
was awarded Officer of the Ord

D1471054

TACKLING DEPRESSION AT WORK

A practical guide for employees
and managers

KERRIE EYERS & GORDON PARKER

Routledge
Taylor & Francis Group

LONDON AND NEW YORK

1 00 599096

First published in Australia in 2010
By Allen & Unwin Pty Ltd

First published in the UK in 2011 by Routledge
27 Church Road, Hove, East Sussex BN3 2FA

Simultaneously published in the USA and Canada
by Routledge
270 Madison Avenue, New York, NY 10016

Routledge is an imprint of the Taylor & Francis Group, an Informa business

Copyright © Black Dog Institute, 2010

Printed and bound in Great Britain by TJ International Ltd, Padstow, Cornwall
Paperback cover and internal illustrations by Matthew Johnstone
Paperback cover design by Lisa White

British Library Cataloguing in Publication Data
A catalogue record for this book is available from the British Library

Library of Congress Cataloging in Publication Data
Eyers, Kerrie.
  Tackling depression at work : a practical guide for employees and managers /
Kerrie Eyers & Gordon Parker.
     p. ; cm.
  ISBN 978-0-415-60171-9 (hbk.) – ISBN 978-0-415-60172-6 (pbk.) 1.
Depression, Mental. 2. Industrial psychiatry. 3. Occupational neuroses. 4.
Employees—Mental health. I. Parker, Gordon, 1942- II. Title.
  [DNLM: 1. Depressive Disorder. 2. Occupational Health. WM 171]
  RC537.E94 2010
  616.89—dc22

                        2010033470

ISBN: 978-0-415-60171-9 (hbk)
ISBN: 978-0-415-60172-6 (pbk)

Contents

Introduction
Some rules of the game

A patient smiled wryly as she described her stay in a psychiatric unit for treatment of her severe depression. 'If I'd broken my leg and been in an orthopaedic ward I would have been surrounded by visitors and flowers. During the two weeks I was in the psych unit I had no visitors, no flowers and no get-well calls from workmates or my boss. When I returned to work, no one asked me any questions or welcomed me back.'

If you have a job and a mood disorder—and with more than 10 per cent of the workforce currently affected, this is a possibility—you can rarely leave it at home, and you can't park it at a Mood-Care Day Centre. As for any physical problem—from the mild and temporary through to the severe and potentially disabling—people bring their medical conditions to work. If they choose to discuss their cold or their heart condition with others, they could expect to receive empathy, interest and support. But observe the difference for a mood disorder. Few risk disclosing it, and those who do often find others' reactions tainted by rejection and discrimination. Such attitudes, of course, also advance the demoralisation and alienation symptomatic of the depression itself.

Reasons for such negative reactions reflect the intriguing perceptual division between physical conditions and mood disorders. Depression and bipolar disorder are physical conditions too, but their presence has to be taken on faith; there is no plaster cast or hacking cough, and the manifestations are psychological—the person is just 'not themselves'.

So why do mood disorders evoke such wary responses? Three reasons, the three Ss—simplification, sensitivity and stigmatisation—stand out. First, simplification. 'Depression', especially 'normal' depression or sadness, is often mild and transient. This risks 'clinical depression' being similarly viewed, even trivialised. The observer may see it as self-indulgence, and overtly or covertly suggest that the individual simply 'snap out of it'. But, for those with significant clinical depression, being told to 'snap out of it' or to 'pull up your socks' is unhelpful and counterproductive. As Matthew and Ainsley Johnstone, co-authors of *Living with a Black Dog*, have observed, 'Socks have little to do with mental health. If people could just "snap out of it" they would. No one ever chooses to have depression.'[1]

Second, sensitivity. Observers are often perplexed about how to respond to someone's very personal psychological pain. As for other private misfortunes (for example, a loss in the family), they pull back from asking how the individual is feeling. Such responses—not questioning, not expressing supportive comments, and avoiding hospital visits—can reflect the observer's concern about appearing insensitive or invading the individual's privacy. However, consider reversing the injunction 'Don't just stand there. Do something!' to 'Don't just do something. Be there.' The observer should not feel that they have to directly raise the topic of depression initially, but indicate by their indirect support and 'being there' that they are aware of the individual's pain. Inquiries, more direct discussion, and assistance and recommendations—where welcome—may follow later.

Third, the mood disorders often evoke stigmatising responses. Why do we stigmatise? The origins probably have evolutionary importance, driven by innate 'survival of the fittest' biological mechanisms that evoke an 'instinctive' reaction against the 'atypical'. Those innate responses may be biologically rational, but are socially and intellectually irrational and—if they become entrenched—lead to the stereotyping and prejudices that continue to drive one group to endlessly seek to suppress another. The psychologist Gordon Allport noted that, while it took years of labour and billions of dollars to uncover the secret of the atom, it would need greater investment to gain the secrets of man's irrational nature—'It is easier … to smash an atom than a prejudice.'

We think Allport was wrong. In the last few decades we have seen such stereotyping modified and, in many cases, overcome. Examples include the improved tolerance and support for physical disabilities, sexual orientation, religious affiliation and gender. Redressing each of those stigmas required a campaign and a set of strategies, as well as a readiness by the community to change mindsets empathically.

Empathy—not sympathy, which is hierarchical—is the capacity for each of us to project ourselves into the life of another person, to identify with them and, if they have some limitation or difference, to begin to understand its nuances.

Thus, when dealing with people with mood disorders, it is useful to be aware that one may need to override any instinctual responses. Over the last decade in Australia, we have observed many highly competent individuals—including politicians and sportsmen—talk comfortably about how they have been 'bitten by the black dog' or have faced the 'rollercoaster' of a bipolar illness. These public figures have been 'culture changers'—creating a climate of acceptance and a better understanding of mood disorders. They have put a 'face' on depression and bipolar disorder, but there are, yet, many other everyday heroes who press on unknown, struggling to manage but too fearful of exposure to seek the support and treatment that would return them to good health and productivity.

The workplace remains a common arena for the themes of oversimplification, sensitivity and stigma to be played out for those with mood disorders. It is weighted to performance, productivity and commitment—there is a 'job' to be done. In reality, the ideal workplace provides much more—it can enhance our self-respect, give us a sense of purpose and satisfaction, enable us to deploy our skills, and offer us a social support system that extends beyond that provided by kith and kin. Such ingredients are not formalised in job descriptions. Instead, the workplace is assumed to operate to a simple model: the workers 'produce' and the bosses ensure high 'performance'.

Understandably, when you add to that mix an individual with a mood disorder that is threatening his or her productivity, then there is strain: the boss sees their mission as being compromised and the individual faces multiple dilemmas—whether to divulge the impact of their mood disorder, try to 'soldier on' or take leave, try to work harder or even seek another job. In addition, the mood state itself (whereby the individual often feels worthless, hopeless and guilty) adds an extra dollop of negativity to the mix. But make no mistake, most employees—if they are in a halfway decent job—value their work and their workplace.

Here, then, is the gap; and it can be bridged. We suggest that both the organisation and the employee struggling with a mood disorder are potentially in accord. They are looking for the same outcome: recovery from the illness and a return to best functioning. For this to happen, the worker must seek help for their mood disorder, take responsibility for it and pursue recovery, and then learn and engage in strategies to remain well.

To encourage this approach and to advance workplace strategies for those with mood disorders, we need to address the three Ss. Government and private workplaces would reap benefits from, first, educating their members about depression and bipolar disorder and offering more sophisticated information rather than a simple model that assumes the word 'depression' to be, by itself, informative; second, providing advice about how to address the sensitivities involved—how, for example, to approach someone struggling with their performance, and support them and provide 'care' without crossing boundaries; and third, advancing destigmatisation of mood disorders in the workplace. By adopting such policies, early recognition and disclosure of depression or bipolar disorder can be fostered, management support formalised, and workplace provisions agreed, thereby setting the scene for effective treatment and a staged return to the workforce or to full work performance.

This book had its origins in the Black Dog Institute's 2008 Writing Competition, 'Tackling Mood Disorders in the Workplace', where we sought the wisdom and observations of those with a mood disorder and of workplace managers about the strategies they had found helpful or counterproductive in the workplace. It joins three earlier companion books (*Journeys with the Black Dog, Mastering Bipolar Disorder* and *Navigating Teenage Depression*) which detail the views of those who have learnt to manage their depression or bipolar disorder, and it moves away from the more usual 'top down' professional-based framework to provide a 'bottom up' or 'shop floor' perspective. We learn from those who have walked the walk. There are many answers, and also better questions, to be explored. Because the mood disorders vary—in type and severity, in degree of impairment and disability, across time, and in response to the demands of work and the workplace environment—it would be sterile and restrictive to produce a bullet-point set of recommendations. We hope that readers can, instead, select pieces of wisdom and advice that they can use to shape their own approach to such issues.

One overriding principle needs emphasis, however. Any workplace can have 'declared' core values, but it is the 'real' core values that are important. What do workers want? At work they seek career satisfaction (a sense of purpose and challenge), support from their seniors (that the boss indicates their worth, respects them and has a value system that can, in turn, be respected), responsive management, and a job that does not eat into their private life. When do they want it? When a worker becomes depressed these issues become even more salient. That is why it is usually preferable for the 'boss' to take responsibility for a depressed employee rather than refer the issue to the human resources department—which is more likely to tackle the problem industrially. Not only will the depressed individual appreciate being supported by their immediate management at a time of personal distress but, when recovered, such treatment will reinforce the individual's respect and commitment to the organisation. What goes around comes around.

There is a 'good news' story from our competition that is worth recording here. One writer described how depression caused her to resign from her job. Her previous employer then came across her essay (circulated to family and friends by her proud husband, as it had won a prize) and she was offered her job back with more flexible hours. There is an old saying, 'You can tell a man's character by what he turns up when offered a job—his nose or his sleeves.' Perhaps this can be reframed to, 'You can pick the real core values of an organisation by observing how management responds to a depressed employee.'

As for our previous books, we hope that the material we have drawn from workers, managers and bosses illuminates the themes and issues. We particularly acknowledge the many astute contributions from our colleague Stephanie Webster. We also would like to thank colleagues from the Black Dog

Institute and the many writers who have generously contributed their stories and observations.

The writer of the following essay took a creative and wistful approach to the Black Dog Institute writing competition, producing an honest 'cover letter' in response to an imaginary job advertisement.

Gordon Parker and Kerrie Eyers

Résumé
To whom it may concern

The Personnel Manager
Every Company
PO Box 123
Industry Park, State 1234

Dear Sir/Madam,

I wish to apply for the position advertised by your company. You will find enclosed my résumé outlining my skills and experience, all of which are impeccable. As you will see, they portray a highly intelligent, multiskilled, proficient employee who can perform any task set. I work well as part of a team or alone, being equally motivated in either case.

I could keep going in this manner, selling myself and my expertise, as a good job applicant does. But like most résumés and job applications, they don't show the whole picture. They are an illusion cleverly woven over fibres of the truth, though those fibres are strong—just as job advertisements do not fully or accurately inform the applicant about the job, the management, the organisation, or any prejudices or politics operating within.

I have been told that, when applying for jobs, your application needs to stand out from the multitudes received. I believe mine will do just this as I give you a more truthful, whole and accurate picture of who I am, my experiences with the world and with my previous employers. Each and every résumé you have received will be full to overflowing with the skills you need. On paper, everyone looks perfect. But we both know that this is not the case and there is more to a good employee than the skills listed on their résumé. By me being honest with you, this sets the stage for a more open and truthful dialogue during interview about the matters I reveal. I will also have some very candid questions for you before I could consider taking a position with your company. This way, neither of us will be wasting time.

You see, I have a mental illness. Chronic 'major depression' with elements of anxiety, to be accurate. And while 'mental health is everybody's business', according to the government campaign, I have not found this to be the case in previous employment. My illness, as with many other conditions, finds me occasionally experiencing periods of time when I am quite unwell. It may require time off for treatment or even hospitalisation. Even during times of relative wellness and stability, I must continue to manage my condition with regular appointments with my specialist team. While my legitimate use of sick leave should not be in question, at previous jobs it was the reason they used to force me to leave. A leading bank, during a period of hospitalisation, demanded I return to work or leave—decision needed now as 'this wasn't good for their reputation'. I had supposedly voided part of my employment agreement about bringing their reputation into ill repute. A doctor I worked for made a similar 'request' of me when I needed time off, despite me not having taken a sick day in three years and my work not suffering at all (he did concede this). Apparently he could not have unreliable and unproductive employees in his line of work. These are not isolated examples. One potential employer terminated an interview when I revealed my condition in answer to her question about medical history. No room for explanation or education. Just 'Leave now, thank you'.

Answering job advertisements is as difficult for applicants as selecting from résumés is for employers, in deciphering what is truth and what is fiction, verifiable qualifications aside. I, though, attempt to answer your questions.

'Is this a year for change?' Life is full of change, but please don't let my depression return so I am no longer the 'dynamic person' this job awaits—depression being a dark force within that clouds my view of the world and saps my energy and motivation. Otherwise, yes, I am an 'energetic person' looking for 'an exciting opportunity' in the 'diverse and flexible role' you are offering. I really hope that I do become part of a 'supportive team environment' with 'approachable and caring management'. How much easier and more pleasant my working life would be, eliminating negative stress and providing me with purpose and fulfilment. These are factors that promote mental wellbeing in everyone, but are essential to someone keeping depression at bay. I am agreeable to having a medical checkup as 'employment is subject to this', as long as discrimination doesn't rear its ugly head and I am deemed unsuitable due to my diagnosis. Having 'hours to suit' me is a great aspect of the employment package. Mostly I will want the same regular hours, as a daily routine helps me manage. But during more turbulent times of illness this will still allow me to come in to work, but just later in the day: depression often improves as the day goes on. With this flexibility I can still be the 'reliable' employee you seek, meeting the 'monthly deadlines' and thus gaining the full benefits of this 'rewarding position'. And you will be gaining an 'experienced and qualified' employee, as my résumé outlines. I am 'eager to take this next step in my career' and know I can do the tasks required for this position 'to a very high standard'. I have a 'sharp and intelligent mind' and learn new material quickly. 'Further training and courses' will be eagerly anticipated by me, as I am 'hungry for knowledge'.

One in five people suffers from a mental illness at some point in their lives, with depression being classed as a mental illness. With 800,000 Australians affected by depression each year, you will find that many people already in your employ are afflicted, as will be many applicants. They just may not have been as open and honest with you as I have been. Around 20 per cent of males and 23 per cent of females in full-time employment have lifetime mental illnesses. The figures are similar for part-time employment. So, depression proves to be no barrier to being a reliable and productive employee. Employment (and productive activity) is actually a major protective factor in maintaining good mental health. These statistics vouch for me, as do my employment history, qualifications and references.

So, you have nothing to lose and everything to gain by choosing me for this position with your company. Depression won't interfere with my work quality and the work will actually assist in keeping me well. Our future liaison will be mutually beneficial. And you already know you are getting an honest person, which goes a long way to demonstrating my good character.

I hope you appreciate my honest, complete and comprehensive application. Being a volunteer Mental Health Advocate in my spare time, as part of my job application I have attempted to educate you about mental illness and reduce some of the stigma surrounding it. I hope I have been successful with this and with my job application, and I look forward to hearing from you with an interview time convenient to us both.

Yours sincerely,
Jane Candoo

1
Sizing things up
The prevalence of workplace disability

'Long gone are the days when we could get away with saying, 'Leave your problems at the door.' We all know that no matter who you are, you usually 'carry *you* around with you' and that most people are not able to separate themselves so that they can come to work without their problems.

Gone also are the days of authoritarian leadership style: this is being replaced by a 'relational' approach to leading, particularly appropriate given that 'depression' is one of the biggest problems facing not only those trying to run a business, but our society as well. The days of the 'do this or you're out' mentality are over, and this calls for a shift in our thinking, attitudes and approaches to managing people, to a cast of mind that looks at and embraces people's needs and can address them.

This does not mean we 'go all soft' and assume responsibility for someone else's life, but it does mean that we look at people in a way that identifies their strengths and weaknesses, then make the most of their strengths, while being able to develop and encourage staff in a way that makes them want to improve the areas that don't work so well. **Alex***

This book is intended for those in the workplace who deal with the effects of depression and bipolar disorder—employers and employees. While there are effective solutions to support workers experiencing difficulties (be they mental health issues or other areas of crisis or illness) and to span the gap between their troubles and the imperatives of the workplace, they are not always straightforward to implement.

---

* In most cases, writers' names and other identifying details have been changed.

Up to one-third of our waking hours are spent in work-related activity. The nature of the work we do, the way that it enables us to use our skills, and our fit with the goals of our workplace are often central in defining how we (and others) view ourselves. Many workers spend more time with workmates than with family. Employment gives structure to our days. The money we earn from selling our skills determines our status and where we fit in the consumer pyramid. Work and wages remind us that other people value us. And the converse: a steady and rewarding job is a protection against mood disorders, while unsatisfactory work or losing one's job are high risk factors for depression.

The effect of unmanaged mood disorders in the workplace strikes at the heart of the implicit professional and social agreement that we enter into with our work colleagues. Lost productivity due to mental illness impacts the 'bottom line' of an organisation, and for the affected individual the struggle to keep pace with their workload is often counterproductive—sometimes fatal. Depression and bipolar disorder exact a high toll in all arenas, but productivity at work is a particular casualty.

How many are affected? The report put together by the World Health Organization, Harvard and the World Bank estimated that in the year 1990 in a disability ranking calculated for males and females of all ages, depression took top place. Bipolar disorder was ranked sixth.[1] Currently, depression is the second-highest-ranking disability for those aged 15–44 years.[2] It manifests in the workplace as absenteeism (not actually getting to work), 'presenteeism' (getting to work but not being able to 'fire up') and erratic work performance.

Subjectively, 40 per cent of those affected state that their depression and bipolar disorder significantly impact on their capacity to contribute to both their work and home life.[3]

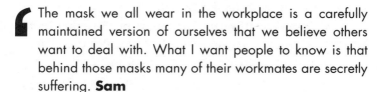

SURVIVING CLINICAL DEPRESSION IN THE WORKPLACE 101
Lecture 1: Handy excuses for odd behaviour
1. Crying at the reception desk:
'I have a touch of hay fever' (particularly salient in the warmer months).
'I have something in my eye' (a cliché but still worth a shot).
2. Wobbly voice on the phone:
'Excuse this cold! I've been coughing for days and now I can't even speak properly.'
3. Extended interludes in the bathroom:
'That curry I had last night is sure giving me grief!'
Meg

AN INVISIBLE BUT REAL HANDICAP

The mask we all wear in the workplace is a carefully maintained version of ourselves that we believe others want to deal with. What I want people to know is that behind those masks many of their workmates are secretly suffering. **Sam**

As noted, more than one in five people in the industrialised West will experience 'clinical' depression at some stage in their life[4], and those aged 25 to 34 feel it worse than most.[5] Add to this the people who develop bipolar I or bipolar II disorder (estimated at between 3 and 10 per cent), with the most likely age of onset being between 18 and 29[6], and it's odds on that there's someone in one of those cubicles or even in the end office who is not up to par today. A survey carried out by the UK Office of National Statistics indicates a prevalence rate of 15.4 per cent for mental health problems among British people in work. On average, nearly one in six of the workforce is affected by clinical levels of depression, anxiety or another mental health condition (around one in five if alcohol and drug dependence are included).[7] In North American estimates, depression affects one-tenth of employees, and depressive disorders account for 30 to 40 per cent of all medical plan dollars paid for mental illness.[8] Current evidence also suggests that the risk of developing a mental health problem, the 'lifetime' risk, may be nearly twice as much as at any other point in history.[9]

Mood disorders don't respect the organisational flowchart: the person coping with depression or bipolar disorder may be at any level in the organisation—including the boss. Prevalence (likelihood of developing a disorder) varies by occupational grade: in a study of employees affected by depression (overall, males 6.2 per cent; females 7.1 per cent), 5.5 per cent of executives rated as affected. Pity the sales people, though, with a prevalence of 10.5 per cent.[10] While many factors operate to cause such differences, the rates clearly reflect potential impact on employee performance and career.

Mood disorders, like other illnesses, fluctuate, remit and show varying responses to treatment. Managers who have been trained in this area are equipped to recognise and deal with distressed employees, setting the boundaries and tone for sympathetic involvement. This leads to a speedier and cleaner resolution, and avoids turning an individual's limitations into a chronic management problem. Skilled intervention and timing clarifies expectations—for bosses, managers and employees—and educates the organisation in effective ways of dealing with similar situations in the future.

Having a psychiatric disorder need not necessarily limit an individual's career. A survey conducted by the Center for Psychiatric Rehabilitation at Boston University found that of 500 professionals with diagnosed psychiatric illness (bipolar disorder, major depression, and schizophrenia), 73 per cent successfully maintained full-time employment in their chosen fields. However, stigma was real—with discrimination that ranged from missed employment opportunities through to workplace colleagues mistakenly attributing normal reactions to psychiatric problems.[11]

THE COST OF UNTREATED MOOD DISORDERS

‘ At work I'm the boss. I answer questions, organise schedules, chair workshops, quote on jobs, hold meetings, check budgets, and listen to, advise on and help with the personnel and the personal. The way people see me is the antithesis of how I feel. To them I'm confident, directed, decisive; to me I'm anguished, anxious, despairing.

When I'm like this I hate being here. I'm cursedly aching to leave. The workday becomes a series of bridges between the sadness that's choked on, the tears held on the trembling edge, the hiding in my office, the willing people away. I use busyness as my protector. The busy walk. The busy desk. For others this translates into 'Only if it's important!' To me it's the same intent but a different reason. I'm wishing them away with 'Don't ask me now. Don't ask me now.'

On better days the work becomes what I can do, a welcome distraction from it all. I use it to pull me out of the malaise, a comforting distraction from what's in my head and at home. Once again the busyness protects me, takes me away from myself and engages me in the world. The flipside of this is that the dissimilarity between work and home forms a divide, and my mood just collapses when the workday ends. **Tran**

The characters on the computer screen swim before me as I stare at them blankly through eyes blurred by a prism of tears—my fist is clenched around a soggy tissue blackened by my mascara. I continually leave my desk to avoid the concerned glances of my work colleagues and lock myself in the toilet where I scrunch up on the floor and break down completely.

After gaining some tenuous composure, I leave this haven and return to my desk in an attempt to bury myself in work requirements. I avoid eye contact and any form of social interaction, but my red, puffy eyes and silent demeanour demand at least one 'Are you okay, Cara?' These four words are the catalyst for another flow of tears.

I suffer from clinical depression and the above events encapsulate a bad day at the office. I am fortunate, though, as I work in a health care environment where I am surrounded by professionals who not only possess the attributes of compassion and empathy but also have an insight into the aetiology and symptoms of depression. It was due to the concern of my supervisor that I was guided to the right place to have my illness first diagnosed and treated.

The support and understanding I receive from those who know of my condition is heartening and this is what has helped me the most. It is an important part of my coping process to know the people I work closely with are aware of the rollercoaster ride that clinical depression can take me on. Not as a ploy to gain sympathy or as an excuse to not carry out the requirements of my job, but to give them an understanding of why there may be days when I am non-communicative and quiet and don't wish to engage in conversation. It is important to me that they know the problem is mine and not theirs. **Cara**

Untreated mental health disorders generate indirect costs through absenteeism and loss of productivity. These are estimated, for American businesses, to be in excess of US$79 billion annually.[12] Six million workdays are lost through depression-related absenteeism each year in Australia—the equivalent of about four days a month—and untreated depression is estimated to account for more than 12 million days of reduced productivity.[13] Depression results in more days of disability than chronic health conditions such as heart disease, hypertension and diabetes.[14]

The recently coined term 'presenteeism' captures a relatively new research area with published work mainly from the US, Canada and Australia. As mentioned, presenteeism describes the class of worker who shows up at work but who then operates at low capacity, procrastinating or just staring at their computer screen for extended periods. It is a sizable problem. In the UK, presenteeism due to mental health problems is estimated to account for one and a half times as much working time lost as absenteeism.[15]

Many of those with mental illnesses are younger members of the workforce. Joseph Calabrese, psychiatry professor at the University of Cleveland, observes that mental illness is highest among 15- to 44-year-olds: 'These people go to work, but they're the working wounded.'[16]

The cost of the lost productivity caused by untreated depression in the general working population has been assessed at A$10,000 per worker and up to A$25,000 for a senior executive or professional.[17] US companies, for instance, lose an estimated US$30–44 billion per year because of employee depression.[18,19]

Bipolar disorder is responsible for even greater lost productivity than is depression: twice as much, according to an American study. Workers with bipolar disorder average 66 lost workdays in a year, compared to 27 days for those with depression. Attendant costs reflect bipolar disorder's more severe depressive episodes rather than its manic upswings.[20]

EARLY RECOGNITION PAYS DIVIDENDS

The UK's Sainsbury Institute for Mental Health posits that improved management of mental health in the workplace, especially prevention and early identification of such problems, could save employers 30 per cent or more of costs attributable to mental illness—at least US$13 billion annually.[21] When an individual obtains treatment in the first few months of a mental illness, early recovery is more likely; and early detection and treatment reduce the chance of the problem becoming chronic—and a workplace issue.

Conversely, when short-term disability is not addressed it can become a long-term issue. In this case, there is less chance that the person is able to assume their previous level of proficiency in the workplace.[22]

In this chapter we have overviewed the societal impact and cost of depression. In the following chapters we move to a more personal perspective.

2
Reading the game
Well-pitched intervention and support

Our team was going through a restructuring and I was having an episode of depression. My manager and I worked out that I would need to check in on a more regular basis to manage the stress. That meant I didn't worry about whether I was focusing on the right things. Other than that, she just let me get on with things as usual. Often you don't need major adjustments.

There were three stages to managing bipolar disorder in my working life:

- needing time off work
- returning to work/maintaining work during an episode
- making long-term choices about my working life.

Stephanie

On return to work I felt stigmatised. The CEO had told the rest of the executive team that I had been in hospital with depression. I felt that my colleagues were looking down on me and sniggering about my incompetence behind my back. The chief financial officer even said to me, 'I don't believe in depression, I think people use it as an excuse to be lazy.' This made me feel isolated and alone. I didn't know who to turn to at work for support. I was the head of human resources. People came to me with their problems and issues but there was nowhere for me to turn. **Ramiro**

People are resistant to disclosing mental health problems, reasoning that it is irrelevant to their job performance and that revealing their condition (if they recognise that they *have* a condition) will expose them to stigma. The capacity to perform at work for an individual with depression or bipolar disorder will range along a spectrum that is also populated

by other people managing a host of life's usual problems—
a new baby, a bad dose of flu, a sick child, the break-up of
an intimate relationship, the development of serious illness.
The partial answer to these scenarios is a well-developed
employee assistance program or, at the least, a well-trained
manager. A sympathetic approach to an employee who is
having problems with work goals and interactions, and
shaping up a game plan together, aligns the expectations
of the person with the problem and the expectations of the
workplace.

Proactive management—involving mental illness destigmatisation, an education campaign, and training for key
managers—has been found to net more productivity for
the organisation and a more contented and open workforce. A ten-year continuing study in the UK found that
people-management practices had the greatest effect—with
a causal linkage between employee motivation and business
profitability/productivity. Comparing similar organisations,
it compared five managerial practices: use of business strategy, emphasis on quality, use of advanced manufacturing
technology, use of research and development, and people
management, with the last having by far the greatest impact
on productivity and profitability. The researchers noted the
benefits of promoting job satisfaction and employee commitment via regular monitoring of opinion and motivation,
and then responding with organisational changes linked to
the annual planning cycle.[1]

As emphasised, early recognition and intervention in workplace issues reaps benefits.[2] The National Institute for Mental
Health (NIMH) in the US has estimated that more than 80 per

cent of depressed people can be treated quickly and effectively. With mood disorders, the key is to recognise the symptoms of depression and bipolar disorder early and then encourage people to receive appropriate treatment.[3] Systematic effort to identify and treat depression in the workplace significantly improves employee health and productivity and leads to lower costs overall for the employer, according to another study funded by the NIMH. In this study, more than 600 employees had been screened and considered to have clinically significant depression. Half of them were then assigned to their choice of active intervention (telephone psychotherapy, face-to-face psychotherapy or antidepressant medication), and the other half were given feedback about their condition and advised to seek care. At a twelve-month follow-up, the group that had had active intervention was 40 per cent more likely to have recovered and 70 per cent more likely to have stayed employed compared to those who had been given passive advice.[4]

STRESS AND ITS EFFECT ON MOOD DISORDERS

❛ As a person with bipolar disorder I can work under pressure to extremely tight deadlines. However, there is a big difference between pressure and stress, and if more people could understand that, work would be a much safer environment. **Patrice**

❛ After working full time with this company for years and having my efforts respected and praised, my world fell apart. I was accepted to a new position within the same company, part time and closer to home. Suddenly there I was, one of two people in a tiny box office without windows. Silence reigned as we tapped at computer keys or answered the phone. After my training phase, any mistake was pointed out with negativity, rudeness and major exasperation with anal repetitiveness. Yes, you guessed it; my new coworker had a strong history of being unable to relate easily to people. Even if I did things correctly but via a different pathway, the result was the same. My already struggling self-esteem eroded as my efforts were constantly put down. Petty rules compounded things. I wasn't even supposed to answer the second telephone in the office because it was used by another department, and answering their phone was not in my job description!

I was determined to ignore the personality traits of my colleague, but the black dog of depression attacked aggressively. After a year in this position, one lunchtime I suddenly crashed. There were no warnings, no incidents to set me off. I just began crying inconsolably. My emotions screamed, 'I just can't do this anymore,' while my brain hollered back, 'Don't be stupid—you are a wimp—you should be able to cope with this.' Like tennis volleys, the self-recriminations flew back and forth until my emotions dragged me down into a vortex of complete ineffectiveness.

Supervisors and managers also have the difficult job of interviewing and matching people to job positions. Put people in the wrong position and difficulties will be created. Since my personality is outgoing and friendly, I could ignore my associate's behaviour when situated in an open office area, but when we were moved to a small, three-desk room, there were no barriers to protect me from his abrasive nature. **Haley**

Stress is a very personal thing. Some people thrive on dead-lines and fast decisions; others wilt. One person's quiet catch-up day at work is another's recipe for terminal boredom. Having said that, there are stressors that will ultimately buckle the most resilient, and some workplace settings are toxic. As production goes global, workplaces may find it diffi-cult to cushion their employees against economic upheavals. It may be that the organisation is forced into delivering more product in less time or with fewer 'human resources'; hence the adage, 'Don't adjust your screen, there's a fault in reality.'

Employers in developed countries, however, have a legal duty to provide a workplace that is safe. This includes mini-mising the risk of stress.

Studies of work-related stress and depressive disor-ders confirm that there are increasing demands from the workplace, coupled with lower job security.[5] Stress is bi-directional, with poorly designed work environments leading to stress and mental health problems, and with workers with mood disorders being less-than-ideal workers while experiencing an episode of depression or a bipolar high. An Australian analysis of workers suffering from depression indicated about 15 per cent had their depressive episodes primarily triggered by job stress, and job stress was found to double the risk of depression. More women than men experienced job stress, and job stress was more likely in lower-skilled occupations.[6]

In some cases there can be medico-legal ramifications. An organisation may be judged liable if a manager or worker develops psychological difficulties in a stressful work envi-ronment. As yet, it has not been determined what degree of work stress (responsibilities, hours worked) may be likely to cause psychological impairment—there is no reliable quantification. As increased work hours become the norm this also adds confusion. But stress-related disability claims by American employees have doubled, according to a recent finding.[7] The American Institute of Stress estimates the cost to industry of stress-related breakdown at US$200–300 billion a year.[8]

But who takes responsibility for the stress exposure? Is stress-related disability driven by the employer or the employee? And what is the responsibility, if any, for the employee who through their own personality characteristics (perfectionistic, ambitious) drives themselves to breakdown?

OCCUPATIONAL GROUPS REPORT THEIR STRESSORS

In general, workers report the main causes of stress at work to be job insecurity, understaffing, random interruptions, email overload, increasing workloads, workplace politics, longer hours and poor management practices. They are also frustrated if they have no say in the way their work is organised, if they are not provided with the material or information to enable them to get the work done, and if decisions are imposed from above without any discussion. New time-saving computer systems that have made offices more efficient have been found to accelerate deadlines and demand quicker decisions, which actually make work more stressful. Computer systems have also changed the way that businesses are organised and this in itself affects the people working within them.

A survey looked at the perceived stressors affecting differing occupational groups ('blue collar' or manual; 'white collar' or professional; and the 'helping' professions). Blue-collar workers reported becoming stressed by lack of control over their work, unsuitable jobs, poor workplace relations and industrial noise. White-collar workers cited interpersonal conflict at work, job insecurity, high demands/low support, an imbalance between work effort required and occupational reward, work pressure, lack of autonomy, and role ambiguity. For those in helping professions, stressors included work demands with poor support, the work environment, low autonomy, lack of control and resources, ambiguity about authority, lack of social support, poor staffing levels and, in some settings, low satisfaction with clients. All found that specific acute events such as negative work relationships, conflict, abuse, harassment, bullying, trauma and long hours worked were stressful. Interestingly, the support of a supervisor, but not of a colleague, helped.[9]

So-called 'job strain'—low job control and high job demands—is linked to a two- to three-fold increase in the risk of depression and anxiety in working men and women: almost one in six cases, according to one study. This association is not explained by social class or personality.[10]

In essence, 'work stress' has multiple causes—both independent and interdependent, both contributed to by personal workplace factors—and manifested in multiple ways, including depression.

3
When someone's off their game
Signals that indicate a problem

SYMPTOMS AND SIGNS OF DEPRESSION

If I wasn't crying in a meeting, I was crying in the elevator or at my desk. Tears would drip into my sandwich. **Maria**

I was sharp all right but as my high gathered force I was transitioning from an extremely effective and assertive communicator into a borderline aggressor who hit on everything and everyone that crossed my self-righteous and omniscient path. **Gerald**

When depressed, I sit at my desk and I despise every single person in this office. Every word, every cough, sniff or sneeze seems designed to irritate me. I burn with irrational anger and I appear snappy, rude and distant to those around me. **Asa**

Google 'bipolar disorder' and the first response you get is a list of celebs who suffer ... The average bipolar sufferer is getting off the train in front of you at the station. We are family members, we are friends and workmates. We tile floors, we drive taxis and we process insurance claims. **Eitan**

Depression is the term used when a severe 'down' period has persisted for more than two weeks and is hindering the ability to function at work and home. Depression is more severe than the 'blues'. Depression is attended by a pervasive sad or empty mood, feelings of hopelessness and pessimism, loss of self-regard, an inability to feel pleasure or to 'fire up', decreased energy and concentration, and sleep disturbance.

There may also be difficulty concentrating, remembering and making decisions, as well as irritability, crying, eating disturbances, and chronic aches and pains. While some people may have only a single bout of depression, others suffer recurrent episodes.

At work, 'telltale signs [of depression] include coming in late, leaving early, avoiding social contact, withdrawing (often to toilet cubicles), not participating in meetings and taking a lot of time to get a job done. Also, physical changes are common—feeling tired, lacking energy and not being able to concentrate. Many males try to manage their symptoms with drugs and alcohol.'[1] There may also be absenteeism, tearfulness, excessive anger, overreaction to situations, morale problems, lack of cooperation, and safety risks and accidents.

EFFECTS OF DEPRESSION AT WORK

For over a year I sat at my desk, often with silent tears rolling down my cheeks, devastated this had returned, determined I was going to beat it. After seven years of study, and casual and temporary employment, I had worked hard to get back to this level, I deserved it, and now I was at risk of losing it all. Sleep was elusive and I couldn't eat. Concentration was impossible. I could barely read what was in front of me.

My boss seemed pleased with my work but nothing reassured me. While I did the job robotically my insecurity ensured strict attention to detail. I was too afraid of being criticised to make mistakes; too afraid of losing this job I had worked so hard for. There were times my boss was clearly puzzled when I did not remember conversations or decisions that had been made just days previously, but I doubt she ever wondered why.

Because I work part-time, assumptions were made about my financial situation. Presumably I must be financially able to afford to work part-time. Gradually it became clear I had a limited income and lived an austere life. Although my boss never asked me outright, I knew her curiosity was aroused. Why would I only work part-time if I didn't have any money? Why would I not want a great social life like she was used to? What did I do with all my spare time? It was the judgements being made that hurt the most, but I could not tell the truth, I could not defend myself. **Kath**

I was at work from the time the security guard opened the front door at 7 a.m. to well after dark. My advice to those pleased managers out there who see a super-keen but clearly half-dead employee is that workaholism isn't always indicative of good mental health. **Soula**

Someone suffering from depression can start to behave out of character, both at home and at work. Depression can seriously impair the individual's ability to work effectively, and they may have to stop work completely for a time in order to recover. Often the impairment is not as acute as this, but it can chronically hinder the individual who attempts to soldier on. Most people battling a depressive episode are very aware that they are not doing their job as well as they used to, and aware that they are working slowly and making mistakes, and often forgetful, irritable and thin-skinned. The affected individual may try to compensate by working, or trying to work, much harder. If they disclose their illness, they worry that even when they have recovered, their job performance will be 'watched' and that any misjudgement they make will be ascribed to the illness and not seen as a mistake that could have been made by anybody. However, if their mood state is recognised and they receive and accept help, it is observed they assume their normal performance at work more readily[2] and some needless distress and disruption to their functioning, and that of the organisation, can be averted.

SYMPTOMS AND SIGNS OF BIPOLAR DISORDER

'I have only ever loved one man with all my heart. Receiving a phone call from him on his mobile at 30,000 feet in first class, informing me that he is Neo from *The Matrix* and that I am to arrange a Porsche to collect him from Heathrow Airport is not a call I wanted to receive, nor could have ever anticipated. The love of my life's slippery slide into mania seemingly took a few hours, but with the cruel gash of hindsight I realised that he had been headed for this moment for months and months.

The fundamental components to his ending up in a north London mental institution were a yearning desire to be wealthy and successful, a burgeoning disappointment in his chosen legal career, a vastly negative 'I'm better than that' attitude, followed rapidly by a period of unemployment, and then burying all these dissatisfactions by smoking marijuana. **Sabina**

Though depression in the workforce is six times more prevalent than bipolar disorder, bipolar disorder, according to a US National Institute of Mental Health study, costs twice as much in lost productivity. The impact (especially the impairment) of bipolar disorder lies more in its severe depressive episodes rather than its manic highs.[3]

For a person experiencing bipolar disorder (once known as 'manic-depressive illness'), moods alternate between depressive lows and manic highs. One sign of an elevated mood is disinhibition—when a person may dress more brightly or seductively, start an affair, speak indiscreetly and overfrankly, and spend too much money on things they don't need. Another sign is becoming too forceful and intrusive, talking more—and over—other people. As one man with bipolar disorder said, 'When I'm "up" I'm up myself—loud, boastful and obnoxious.' Individuals may be 'wired'—full of energy and ideas but often without the capacity to put such ideas into effect. They are easily distractible, and irritated with what seems to them the slow comprehension of others. They show an unshakeable confidence in their often grandiose schemes. They often feel 'at one' with the world and describe mystical experiences. There is a feeling of everything making sense. Their normal day-to-day levels of anxiety seemingly disappear. Libido is increased and many individuals crave alcohol to take their high further. The capacity of personal and collateral damage when someone is high during Friday night after-work drinks or at the Christmas party is often unappreciated, with observers thinking that it is just the 'alcohol talking'. Sometimes, however, it is the high that is shouting.

EFFECTS OF MANIA AT WORK

❝ The principal was my next victim. The head teacher had organised the meeting directly after our rather, shall we say, unproductive, and—particularly on my part—argumentative and adversarial discourse. By now I had left all vestiges of conformity behind and assumed the stance of a rebel who had a cause to remedy all that was, in my view, amiss—with not only the school, but the entire breadth of the education system. I took the opportunity with the principal to highlight some of my concerns. Needless to say she highlighted her own concerns and all of them were targeted at my professionalism. Obviously the woman had personal issues with me because I was the same as I ever was. Wrong.

Only in hindsight did I become fully aware that I had had little or no insight into myself and my sudden metamorphosis into a fiercely feisty fire-breathing female dragon. Shortly after the onset of term recess I began to hallucinate. Sleep deprivation had finally caught up with me. **Margaret**

Someone experiencing a bipolar high might display an overly happy or outgoing mood and/or an extremely irritable mood. Managers and colleagues may become aware that the person is talking very fast and experiencing racing thoughts—jumping from one idea to another. The person is easily distracted, may take on but not complete a lot of new projects, is restless, impatient, driven, 'pumped' and full of energy, and displays an unrealistic belief in their own abilities. Additionally, they may become sexually provocative and indiscreet, behave impulsively and take part in a lot of pleasurable high-risk behaviours—spending sprees, impulsive sex, and unwise business investments.[4]

The following writer describes his 'full circle', but with success in his second round.

❛ HOW I CAME FULL CIRCLE

When you have bipolar disorder, you don't suffer from mania—everyone else around you does. A brief and bizarre one-man party that leaves you with one hell of a hangover called depression. And while those who care for you may feel horrible and helpless, you suffer the depression all alone.

My hangover has lasted far longer than the 'party'. To appreciate my experience with bipolar disorder in the workplace, I have to take you through my gruelling trudge to get back into the workforce. Bear with me, understanding that however difficult it is to read, it's far more difficult to live.

First, you wake up from a brief but harrowing psychotic episode, your head heavy from the drugs that the nurse Ratcheds made you take. You find you've lost your keys, your rights, your independence, your adulthood and your grip on reality. I'd call it rock bottom if I still believed there was one. Shuffling around in hospital slippers, finger painting while the furry-fuzziness in the back of your head gradually subsides, the world is now outside, as unreachable as the end of a rainbow. Getting better, more lucid, they let you go back to your mum's home.

But what now? Reality has been shattered and reconstructed. You're a lost zombie. Sure, you're in familiar surroundings, but in terms of your life, you've been let off at the side of an empty country road, with just an overnight bag and a list of medications to take. A well-meaning outpatient consultant visits once a week, presumably to check up on you, make sure you're not still crazy, but otherwise you have nothing to do. You sink.

Weeks and months slip by. Meds change and gradually you start to feel more human, but inertia has set in. You have come to a complete stop, with nothing to do, no energy or desire to do anything. Life has few fixtures: daytime TV if you can stand it, social security forms, psychiatrist appointments. You have 24 hours in the day to kill. Sleep is the only respite from your annoying life, so that's what you do, as much as you can, till you get to the stage where you don't want to get out of bed in the morning. You have to fight, to physically force the warm, comforting covers off to endure another day. You are fully aware of how pathetic it is and you despise yourself for it. There's no reason to go to the post office, mow the lawn, and eventually you don't see the point of brushing your teeth or showering. You frustrate those who love and care for you and you hate yourself for it. You wake up the next day and it's the same all over again. There's no weekend, no holidays. You derive no pleasure from anything anymore. Movies, dining, socialising are all chores now—cold, overboiled vegetables that you force yourself to eat because they are supposed to be good for you.

What was once recreation is now therapy. The little money you have saved steadily trickles away as you attempt to get out of your house, your rut. You eat for something to do, to fill you up. Together with the medication and lethargy you grow fat and sluggish. Your friendships slip away; you don't belong and your conversation skills get rusty. You come to realise that when you do nothing, you have nothing to talk about. You wish you didn't have to wake up, didn't have to endure your excruciating existence for the sole sake of not hurting your family. You accuse yourself of being too lazy to commit suicide.

So you keep on going, trying, but not believing you can get through the quagmire. You take cognitive behavioural therapy (CBT) classes that irritate the hell out of you, but get you interacting and out of the house. Positive thinking is great, CBT helps many, but when even sunny beaches and puppies piss you off and make you ache because you can't appreciate them, you have little to no patience for the people trying to help you.

Between *Oprah* and the afternoon sitcom re-runs you make a simple call to a rehabilitation service. It is the start of an arduous, tedious and eventually life-saving journey back into the workforce, back into the real world. Suddenly there is someone on your team giving you practical help, setting goals and creating career ambitions for your second life. It's all unimaginable at the time, but something to aim for once you're out of the swamp. You fill out a form; wait a few weeks; attend an interview; wait a few weeks; complete a questionnaire; wait a few weeks; take some classes; wait some more. Finally, after a few phone calls on your behalf, you have a few days of trial work! You feel anxious and finally have a reason to shower and cut your hair, but you've lost your self-esteem, your belief in yourself and your abilities, your confidence. You are just a fragile shoot regrowing and the pressure of starting a new job in the real world is too much. You burst into tears after your first half-day and don't return.

So you change direction. You take a menial, dirty job that fits your state of mind and slowly move towards bigger and better goals. Your rusty mind and flabby body start to dust off and slowly and unsurely get moving. You are an old truck grinding through the lowest of gears; every little thing takes a huge effort, though you're barely moving. At times it feels like you're push-starting a car with square wheels—heave, stop. Heave, stop.

And then, with a little luck, you get accepted into university. With study comes pride, justification, identity and challenge. You get to say you're a student; a well-needed break from just being mentally ill. You get to hide your condition. You meet people who aren't supportive family, doctors or social security officials, so it's no longer written on your forehead. More importantly, you deal with your condition and learn to manage it. You exercise diligently, try to eat right and you go out—not because you want to or feel like it, but because you know you'd feel worse if you didn't. Plus, every now and again, you catch yourself actually having fun. The study is daunting and overwhelming, but a welcome distraction and you relish it. After four years of trudging with no end in sight, the sun is out again, and you can feel it on your face. You've escaped.

Then one day you're doing work experience as part of your study, learning on the job in a hospital, a budding health care professional in training. You're reading up on a patient's case notes with your supervisor, to prepare for a first visit, when out of the blue you see a shockingly familiar term on the page: the patient has bipolar disorder. You then see your supervisor groan and roll his eyes—'These ones are always a handful,' he says, knowingly. You feel the pangs of prejudice deep in your stomach, but you don't say anything. You see the patient, try to articulate your silent empathy with understanding eyes and a friendly smile. But you don't say anything. You feel shame at not speaking up, a fraud, but also unnerved that after coming so far away from your condition, feeling like you've finally shaken the monkey from your back, it comes up and confronts you head-on again.

So that's how I came full circle to experience bipolar disorder in the workplace. But the truth for me is that bipolar is something that I will always have and will always have to deal with. Though I'm off all meds and stable now, I still see my psychiatrist regularly and know my early warning signs. I'm not yet comfortable talking about it or trying to be a role model, and I don't have to be, not yet anyway. The way I see it, I'm still learning my trade and I need to be seen as a professional first. Once I have gained expertise and respect in my profession, then I will be in a position to discuss depression and bipolar disorder with my colleagues, to challenge mainstream opinions and provide insight from both sides of health care. This is what I resolve to do. In the meantime, I am in a unique position to work with patients who experience depression or bipolar disorder—to offer respect, dignity and real understanding. **Nick**

4
Early intervention scores goals
Managerial strategies

EMPLOYER CONCERNS

A simple application for sick leave through my superannu-ation fund, and a later claim for workers' compensation, led me through a dirty quagmire of psychiatrists' reports that regarded me as some sort of object to be questioned on integrity and presentation, and were full of innuendos. Official reports to my employer have included comments suggesting that I am casually attired, have unkempt hair and am somewhat disingenuous. These reports were made available to me, as well as to employers, union representatives and lawyers. My husband initiated legal proceedings on my behalf, as I lacked the energy and willpower required. As I write this, five years later, my person—all that is me, defines me and describes me—is being scrutinised by officials in tall empty buildings who have the audacity to question the person I know as me.
Patricia

While early intervention is advocated for a mental health problem that is beginning to incapacitate an individual in the workplace, actually implementing this may be quite another story. Mental health problems are often not recog-nised or acknowledged by the individual suffering from them, and few consult a general practitioner. The WORC (Work Outcomes Research and Cost-benefit) project being carried out in Australia indicates that less than 25 per cent of those with depression are receiving treatment and a further third of people with diagnosable levels of mental illness don't admit to having any condition.[1]

Some employers fear that if they start mental health initi-atives and adopt a more accepting culture in their workplace, it will lead to false claims appearing 'out of the woodwork'. This has not been the case for the organisations that the group Mental Health @ Work has been engaged with over time. There is much reliable evidence demonstrating that it is preferable for organisations to have employees seek treatment, and this has been shown to improve productivity.[2] One example is GlaxoSmithKline in the UK, which has, since 2002, implemented a 'resilience program' that they estimate has reduced work-related mental illness by 60 per cent, and decreased absence associated with such illness by 29 per cent over three years.[3]

Employer and organisation concerns about 'depression' or other mental illnesses in the workplace may reflect views about diffuse concepts and their many different manifestations. The range can include the conscientious and gravely ill worker or manager who makes a good recovery, through to the worst-case scenario of someone who is managing their disorder poorly, impacting on others (for example, through irritability, unreliability and overflow work) and with no time-frame for treatment or recovery. In some cases, poorly handled depression can start to look like 'entitlement' on the part of the employee and any workplace accommodations seem to other members of the workforce to be special treatment. The most common scenario is that an employee's performance has deteriorated and yet they are unwilling to disclose their condition. In any of the above situations, widely disseminated policies about performance criteria and employee entitlements can clarify expectations for all parties involved.

An additional concern for the organisation (and the employee!) is the unpredictability of depressive and bipolar illness. For example, how long will the episode last? How severe and how recurrent is it likely to be? An assessment of job performance in workers with depression, funded by the US National Institute of Mental Health, noted that 44 per cent of their sample of people with depression were already taking antidepressants when they began the study and yet still met clinical criteria for depression, and that their job performance continued to suffer despite some clinical improvement.[4] The researchers recommended that depression treatment should be aimed at remission and that health professionals need to pay more attention to recovery of work function and development of workplace supports. Additionally, well-thought-through organisational policies about levels of support and measurable recovery milestones ensure less misunderstanding for both employers and employees.

Work environments also vary widely. Is there a human resources department or an Equal Employment Opportunity (EEO) policy? Is it a small business? What is the person's relationship with their manager like? Are they a casual worker or a long-term employee; junior or senior; on a career path? What is the culture like? Is there a lot of stigma attached to disclosing a mood disorder in the work environment?

Generally, an employer or organisation is expected to make some accommodation to enable an employee to function in the job during or on recovery from depression or bipolar disorder. The extent of such changes to the workplace and the job tasks are balanced against whether they are reasonable workplace adjustments. If the employer is unable to implement such changes—due to the size of change needed to fit the employee back into the organisation—

then, at some point, the employer can claim unjustifiable hardship.

Employee advocates recognise that, ultimately, an employee is required to be able to carry out their job. If an employee cannot function in the job after reasonable provision of workplace support, then they are unable to meet the inherent conditions of the job. It may be that the person affected by a mood disorder is working in a job that is not a good match for them and that they could deploy their skills better in another area more suited to their temperament and skills, for instance a less stressful arena, or that the organisation could accommodate a change to job-sharing or contract work. Finding the right 'ecological niche' for an individual in the workforce can be a very useful temporary or ongoing strategy.

REASONABLE WORKPLACE ADJUSTMENTS

'This job is all I could hope for. I work for an organisation where employee wellbeing is a priority. We look out for, and after, each other. My manager knows about my life and family and asks after them. Different teams organise a weekly morning tea, an unhurried opportunity to share and debrief which is always well attended. Once a month, a massage therapist is onsite offering twenty-minute appointments. There is an active and enthusiastic social club, an anti-bullying committee, an employee health committee and a range of flexible work arrangements. Individual and team supervision sessions are a normal part of the working week. Staff are encouraged to access professional support for work or personal issues through the EAP (employee assistance program), and anyone involved in a traumatic event is automatically offered Critical Incident Stress Debriefing. A complimentary fruit bowl, a walking group and a Pilates class after work encourage healthy options. Emails regularly circulate with links to sites on nutrition, stress management, exercise and mental health.

It is simplistic to think that any one of these features of my workplace can prevent a mood disorder, but collectively they create a strong culture of care and connection within the organisation. In this environment the process of asking for help is normalised, encouraged and without stigma. The message is clear: we value you and we want you to be healthy and whole. **Ella**

What would have improved the situation during my period of depression? What strategies could have been put in place to help me? I'd have liked the manager to show me some concerned interest. At that time, work was the only stable base I had. Of course I didn't want to let them all down like that. But I needed some assistance and support if I was going to get the job done, like, perhaps, moving my work space to a quieter area or working different hours or having other people take the phone calls. Maybe I could have undertaken different duties for a while? Or my work targets could have been reduced temporarily. These are simple adjustments in the workplace which can help. **Riley**

While an organisation will go out of business if it cannot meet the 'bottom line', there is a continuing debate about increasing hours spent at work and the greater insecurity of contract jobs, and the influence that these two factors have had on employee expectations and loyalty to any particular place of business. However, if any employee regularly arrives late for work, even after job and workplace adjustments have been made, or if the employee cannot function in the job even after reasonable adjustments, then this is a job performance issue. An organisation is not required to offer a different job to the employee or to create a new job for them.

Employers have responsibilities to personnel, so there is an expectation that some adjustments will be made to the workplace environment if this is likely to assist the employee. Adjustments might include helping an employee to deal with their role and their interaction with others, establishing checklists and goals, and helping them to manage their time, punctuality and attendance. It can be necessary for the employee to avoid shift work, and they may 'trade' their shifts with others in return for some favour from them. The employer might also offer more flexible working hours to enable visits to a mental health professional, arrange shift or location changes, reduce workload or particular tasks, offer mentoring, coaching, peer support (or peer worker mentoring—assistance from a person from outside the workplace who has recovered from a mood disorder), and, particularly, provide general education to all employees about mental health in the workplace. A regular meeting with the supervisor can deal with any problems before they become serious or chronic. In most cases such accommodations are inexpensive and involve workplace flexibility rather than capital expenditure. Such arrangements and support may also be temporary and only required, for instance, to assist a person's return to the workplace after recovery from illness.

Adjustments to the workplace environment might include providing the employee with a tape recorder to tape instructions from supervisors, training programs and meetings if they have difficulty with memory; the use of a desk lamp to minimise the flicker of fluorescent lights; allowing the use of headphones to protect from loud noises; modifying their work space or changing location to a quieter area where an employee will be free from distractions; or allowing them to work at home.

One crucial adjustment needs to happen to the work environment—stigma is stressful and counterproductive and demeans all. Fellow workers often take their cues about the organisational culture from management. If managers show trust and respect to someone with a mood disorder, this flows on. If tolerance has been a part of regular training, it will be easier for the manager to support someone who has returned from leave and to answer the questions about them, or address complaints about the accommodations which others may see as special treatment. Each issue needs to be managed—a balance of 'support' versus 'special treatment', and confidentiality versus openness.

MANAGEMENT CONCERNS

My manager asked me into the vacant staff lunchroom for a one-on-one. It didn't go well. For every attempt on her part to establish why my attitude and demeanour had changed, I denied that any change had arisen.
Margaret

Despite my best efforts, depression makes me an inconsistent performer at work. I know I confuse my boss. Why, at times, do I deliver enthusiasm, ideas and profits in equally high measure, and why, at other times, do I become difficult and unresponsive? **Pete**

Get up, you have to iron some clothes, you have a meeting tomorrow. I can't, I'll do it in the morning. Get up and have a shower. I can't, I'll do it in the morning. Tomorrow morning never comes. I can't get out of bed, what's the use. Turn off your mobile phone; don't log in to your laptop. If you don't get out of bed, you'll be sacked. I can't. What about your presentation? I can't.

One day passes. Turn on your phone. Hell! Five messages, one of them to ring your boss.

I see the boss the next day. He asks me if there is anything wrong as I have had an unusually high number of sick days compared to the rest of the managers in my department. I break down and tell him I think I have depression as I can't stop crying, and I lock myself in my room and I live in a permanent state of despair. I explain that I don't know why, as I have a great job and really enjoy it.

He is surprised, as my work has been very good and I have delivered on all the projects to date this year. To look at me, he said, he would never have known there was anything wrong with me. He has a mother who had depression and so he understands, and suggests that I take a week off and go and see a doctor and get some treatment, as he doesn't want to lose me. **Gary**

A MANAGER'S POINT OF VIEW

Managing a member of staff with depression isn't easy, but I always try to remember that the experience of depression is many times more challenging for the person involved. I've tried to ensure there is a supportive environment, and that means being flexible in looking at workload, finding ways to minimise work-related stress, being available to talk, being non-judgemental and just being aware of signs when something is wrong. But it is perhaps the flow-on consequences that are the most difficult to manage. The heaviness and blackness of depression can sometimes be felt by others—affecting the general mood of a department. I've not really found a way to deal with this, other than to keep an eye out to ensure that everybody else is managing and to be as equally supportive to them. Nobody is immune from experiencing depression, but I do believe an empathetic workplace can help ease some of the personal burden and help sufferers recover their sense of worth. This can only work to the benefit of an organisation. **Nicola**

MANAGEMENT-DRIVEN IMPROVEMENT TO THE WORKPLACE

Managers' decision-making styles range from directive—where decisions are made by the manager and announced to staff, or the manager makes the decision and then 'sells' it to the staff—through to more collaborative approaches, which include inviting staff contribution to a decision but with the manager retaining authority to make the final decision or inviting staff to join the manager in making the decision.

Decisions can also be delegated to another party (for instance, management consultants).

Characteristics of managers who craft a rewarding workplace environment include the capacity to:

- demonstrate that they appreciate each person's contribution
- help staff to feel that they are part of something bigger than themselves and their individual job
- share the most important goals and direction for the group and make them measurable and observable
- trust the intentions of people to do the right thing and make the right decision
- give access to the information needed to make effective decisions
- assist staff decision-making by asking questions, and not by telling them what to do
- share some of the 'perks' of the office, for instance, allow staff to attend arenas where there is decision-making and influence, or allow staff to get some of the limelight
- provide frequent feedback (both reward and recognition, and constructive criticism)
- avoid blaming staff, and when a problem occurs, ask what is wrong with the work system rather than what is wrong with the person
- encourage communication by listening to staff.[5]

A key support for managers is provided when mental health is embedded into a wider health and wellbeing plan endorsed by the organisation. Workplace programs support the manager to recognise the signs of stress and mental illness in an employee and train them to intervene sensitively. Problems at work can be treated as a workplace performance issue. The manager can then go on to provide a supportive structure to clarify expectations of both the worker and the workplace and refer the worker on to the necessary professional help.

Warning signs of mental illness that may alert managers include:

- constant late arrivals or frequent absences
- general inability to cooperate or work with colleagues
- decreased productivity or increased accidents and safety problems
- complaints of fatigue, unexplained pains, difficulties in concentrating, making decisions or remembering things
- poor work, frequent missed deadlines and attendant excuses
- decreased interest or involvement at work, or excessive overtime
- strange or grandiose ideas, displays of anger, irritability and blame.

Managers who are approachable and supportive of staff are the bedrock of an organisation. Hopefully the in-house attitudes to any disability enable them to effectively manage an employee who is unwell. They need the skills and authority to be able to monitor, to timeline, to identify any additional supports needed, to stage any time off required by the worker, to decide a return date and to modify the job environment as much as is realistic. Training in this area helps managers to understand boundaries and be able to handle such problems without pep talks, accusations or gratuitous curiosity.

If the organisation is large enough, the human resources officer or those managing any employee assistance plan can outline the legal obligations owed by the organisation to an impaired worker, so that everyone is clear from the start about the obligations owed by both sides. All plans, agreements and timelines should be documented, and appropriate records given to the employee for their file. Exceptions (for instance, where confidentiality may be at risk) can be complicated and, ideally, rare.

Managers can:

- identify mood swings
- keep a record of performance problems and back this up with specific instances
- use such a record for early intervention (thus increasing the chance of a positive outcome)
- discuss types of support with the employee and coordinate with appropriate professionals
- mutually decide any job support needed, what is possible and how to implement it
- reorganise resources to minimise the impact of an employee's illness on other workers
- timeline the agreed-on plan—include 'feedback loops' and follow-up, then review progress, using suitable performance indicators.

MANAGING REINTEGRATION STRATEGIES

A planned gradual return was implemented that not only addressed my hours of work but also my duties. Bit by bit as my confidence was regained I took back more responsibilities until I returned to full capacity. **Raefe**

I commenced back at work on half days to enable me to attend appointments, to exercise and to rest. I then gradually increased my hours and worked full days. **Prakesh**

In retrospect, how lucky it was that I was working for the public service. I was offered a graduated return to work, and was transferred to what was assessed as a stress-free workplace. Initially I worked a three-day week, increasing gradually to four days and then to a full working week. **Tony**

We devised a 'wellness plan', which allowed me to manage my illness and incorporate my work responsibilities into this plan. **Fidelma**

The manager will generally be responsible for reintegrating the recovering worker back into the workplace. Procedures include setting benchmarks—that is, realistic goals and standards based on the needs of the organisation and the employee's current abilities—and then follow-up. Attaining clear, defined goals is a useful way for the employee to rejoin the workplace. Reintegration may be staged, and, depending on the job and on the organisation's resources, may begin with sending an employee work at home or having them return part-time.

How did my illness affect my work performance? When hypomanic I imagined myself to be more empathic with patients, but this was rarely so, as my overtalkativeness, cavalier attitude, bonhomie and irritability alienated them. One private patient was so concerned by my pressure of speech and distractibility that she contacted the medical board. Occasionally, mild hypomania in me was a useful tonic for a depressed patient. I had heightened and unrealistic perceptions of my diagnostic and therapeutic prowess. Prognoses could be blighted by over-optimism. I was much less willing to consider the opinions of colleagues on diagnostic and management issues if they were contrary to my own. Clearly, both hypomanic and depressive episodes also worsened staff relationships in manifold ways.

When moderately to severely depressed, there was a paucity of speech, ideas and clinical notes. Diagnosis and management was now restricted and narrow, two-dimensional if not shoddy. My low spirits and pessimism were patently counterproductive for the majority of patients, whether they were beset by depression or most other psychiatric disorders (barring depression being an antidote for hypomanic patients!). Lack of self-confidence and unassertiveness meant that, for example, challenging issues were not confronted. I was slow, pedestrian and uninspired. Procrastination reigned.

Although this is primarily a personal account of my bipolar disorder, I believe that it is objective and that it highlights the problems of untreated illness in a doctor's workplace for sixteen years, both as a registrar and as a private sole practitioner. My experiences are likely to be akin to those of other community leaders, such as businessmen, lawyers or politicians, who are either self-employed or in positions of such power that they are effectively quarantined or isolated, so that serious affective illness goes undiagnosed, recognised but ignored, or untreated, with the risks of personal catastrophes, such as adverse outcomes for patients and clients, being disbarred from practice, murder–suicides, or community losses such as companies going bankrupt or political leaders launching warfare. **Jake**

If the boss, manager or employee doesn't know or refuses to acknowledge that they have a mental health problem, there may be little that can be done to help them. Confining focus to work performance is seen to be the best approach, and if performance has not improved by set times, and there has been no request for accommodation or leave, then it becomes appropriate to consider other organisational options.

5
Managing time out
Mental illness and its knock-on effects

> Having a mood disorder is not your fault. But it is your responsibility. Taking charge is the first step towards mastering it. **Margaret**

> People with mood disorders have the right to work, but I think it is also our responsibility to find ways to maintain our mental health and wellbeing. **Pam**

Functional groups evolve in a healthy and efficient workplace, being based on informal social contracts. Though, primarily, the employee 'sells' their services to a company in return for wages, there are generally deeper attachments to the organisation—social and structural benefits that go beyond the satisfaction of exercising our work skills. Thus, disability—of any sort—affects not only the individual but his or her colleagues and the workplace. The difficulty is that mood disorders have psychological manifestations which make an individual sensitive and defensive. This results in reluctance on the part of the manager or the boss to address aberrant workplace behaviour for fear of saying the wrong thing, invading privacy or making things worse. The affected person exemplifies a paradox: they may lack the insight or conviction that they are ill, yet it is their responsibility to seek ways to get back to optimal functioning—to find what will get them well and then what will keep them well. As the saying goes, 'You alone can do it, but you cannot do it alone.'

If they feel they are not coping, an employee owes it to themselves and others to seek advice from someone they trust. Do they, indeed, have a problem? What is it and what are some solutions? In both Canada and Australia, studies report that only about one-third of people with depression seek help.[1,2] For people who have had previous episodes of depression or bipolar disorder, there are likely some supports in place already. During an earlier episode they may have devised creative ways of managing the condition and appointed others to be their 'outside insight' reference— a role that involves spotting the early warning signs of an approaching relapse and then effecting agreed-on strategies to avoid or minimise the episode.

When an employee decides to discuss problems and stressors in the workplace with their boss or manager, it is helpful if the person affected can focus on solutions or accommodations that can help them overcome their present difficulties. A trade union or professional association may become involved at this point. There are also job coaches and peer supporters who may be of assistance. As discussed, if the organisation is large enough there may be an employee assistance program or personnel in human resources to lead the way—although one might argue against involvement of human resources, as such a department is required to meet legal rather than necessarily personal priorities.

Once the accommodations and other provisions have been made, however, the employee should be able to meet all relevant job requirements and standards. It is worth emphasising that documenting plans and progress is important. Of course, some jobs are not able to be modified. They are inherently stressful and people self-select for them: the futures trader, the air traffic controller … Here the ideal solution for the individual who is experiencing stress and/or depression is to find a more suitable position elsewhere.

Sometimes the employee benefits from workplace mentoring, for instance in cases where an employer can only see poor workplace performance and assumes the employee has a bad attitude or is intentionally being difficult. Here, the employee—perhaps in company with a supportive other—may be able to outline for the employer the behaviour that is part of their illness, and map out suggestions about what they are able to do to improve the situation and what might be able to be changed in the workplace to help them manage better.

On the following pages, one writer describes how she manages her ongoing bipolar disorder.

 Q: WHAT DID YOU FIND WAS BEST FOR YOUR RECOVERY?
A: I went back to work as quickly as possible
During my first two episodes I suffered from very severe depression. I had eight months off work the first time. I then had a second episode about eight years later. I tried to work through it, but completely hit the wall, and quit my job. In fact, someone quit it for me because I was too sick to even get there, let alone speak to anyone. Then, the way things turned out, I needed just six weeks off. Really, I should have asked them for leave. I have since told my family never to let me quit a job while depressed.

I went on lithium around the time of my third episode, and my depressions became much, much more manageable—probably a 50 per cent improvement. The most distressing symptoms (suicidal thoughts and major problems with sleeping/eating/concentration) went. Negative thinking, anxiety and a grinding fatigue remained the main challenges. I could do just about anything through those milder depressions though, even presentations. I just went home and collapsed at the end of each day.

Fairly recently, another medication was added in, which has taken my depressions away altogether. After six—often lengthy—depressions. Hallelujah!

Funnily enough, that created fresh challenges. I now have to learn how to prevent or manage mild but fairly frequent mood elevations. I get them more often pre- cisely because I am never in the depressed phase. They completely stuff up my concentration for a couple of days, which is an incredible nuisance from a work point of view. So, twelve years on, I'm still working on the balanc- ing act.

I found being in work really valuable in the recovery process because of:

- routine
- removing the anxiety associated with loss of income
- less opportunity for negative self-talk
- necessary interaction with people
- confidence from hanging in there
- money to socialise
- additional funds for extras for health, such as gym membership, yoga, massage
- ability to afford private health insurance and medications.

I am still learning that I should take time off for mania

I am 'lucky' with my manias. I notice them myself and I respond quickly to medication and schedule a day off when they occur. Working from home at this time is another excellent strategy. When you are elevated, you can hear a pencil drop from five offices away and it's hard to stay focused.

Q: HOW DID YOU GET BACK INTO THE WORKFORCE?

A: Initially, I swallowed my pride

I was prepared to do things like work as a temp, work at a lower level, work in new environments and work for less money. However, I was always prepared to leave a job if there was some sort of chronic stress in the environment, a particularly difficult manager for example. While not glamorous, these steps all helped create a pathway back to work for me. My first episode was very serious. Not everyone will need to make compromises like these.

It was a trial and error process to find the right recovery job. In the twelve to eighteen months following the first episode, I tried several different types of work. My first was a foray into hospitality that lasted just two hours. I worked out that having to smile all day at customers was not going to be possible while I was depressed. Then I did a really easy office job for a few weeks (a temp job). I waited another month and then I got work in the recruitment industry. The hours were pretty long and there was no lunch break. I actually quite liked making phone calls and going out to see clients (which I guess plays to my strengths), but I found it hard to work in an environment where people were competing against each other (sales). I also found it hard to keep up with the social life that the job entailed. At that stage of my recovery I just needed to go home and collapse.

In the end, the travel, the hours and the social pressure wore me down. My health wasn't improving. I resigned and went to work in a banking environment again, but in an administrative position. This time the hours were reasonable and it was definitely not a pressured job. In fact, there were days when there just wasn't enough to do. It was also the first of many roles where I learnt that the qualities that make you suitable for professional work are not always appreciated in more junior positions. If you showed initiative it could easily be misinterpreted as trying to undermine your manager. So the combination of a petty manager and a boring job made me move along after a while.

I found the middle ground with the next job. It was in the banking environment but had lots of client contact. It was still junior enough to give me reasonable hours, but was frenetic during the day (which kept my busy mind busy). I enjoyed working with colleagues who were all selected for client-facing roles. They were not competitive with each other. They were friendly and supportive. It was a large investment bank, so there was also the opportunity for me to get more involved career-wise.

Q: WHAT COPING MECHANISMS DO YOU USE AT WORK CURRENTLY?

A: I now respect my limitations and I have a reasonable sense of where my boundaries are, health-wise. I also operate to the following:

I try to work to my strengths

Having had different work experiences (during my recovery) has helped me identify my strengths in a way that I don't think would have occurred if I had just stayed in one type of job. I now look for work that plays to these strengths.

Initially, I was careful with my working hours

In my early recovery, working a standard nine-to-five day was really important. That daily structure was helpful, and so was the reasonable number of hours. These days I can work longer hours if I have some flexibility, like some control over when and where I work. I do try to keep it reasonable though. I would never, ever do shift work, even now.

I saw a psychologist

When I was recovering from my first episode I saw a psychologist who used cognitive behavioural therapy (CBT). That was incredibly helpful in learning to manage the negative self-talk that goes with a severe depression.

I use my family's support

The best thing that a family member has done for me while I have been working full-time and still recovering from depression is to drive in and pick me up at the end of each day. There were times when getting through the day was a major ordeal. It was wonderful knowing that there would be a friendly face to meet me at the end of it and I didn't have to muster the energy to deal with public transport. A lunchtime phone call helps, although sometimes email is better if there is a risk of feeling emotional. Being let off the housework is also brilliant.

I cocoon

When you are working full-time with depression, you are already giving 100 per cent of what you've got during the working week. I need to collapse on the weekend and spend at least one day in pyjamas doing absolutely nothing. Friends and family have to let you opt out of social arrangements until your energy levels adjust to your job.

I keep an eye on self-medication
When I am working and depressed, it is a real challenge not to use alcohol as a reward or to use it to take the edge off the depression. I'm good now, but in the early stages of recovering it was very easy to get into bad habits.

I make lists
When I am depressed I become a list maker because I have concentration problems. I write everything down and then I make sure I do at least a few things every day to get through the list. Then I can sort of relax—if it's on the list, then I will get to it. If I have done a few things on the list, I can feel that I have achieved something, that life is moving along slowly.

I organise my work
I try to do the worst jobs early in the day so that I don't dread them all day. I tend not to want to talk much with colleagues, so I just put my head down and work really hard. I tend to be more productive when I am depressed. I usually feel that I am not doing a good enough job, so I really push myself. I don't do any overtime or go to work functions, though.

Sometimes, I just fake it
Once I had recovered from depression a couple of times, I knew that you actually do recover. For a while there, my depressions were lasting four months each, so I sort of knew when things would turn around. Managing at work through an episode really became about faking my way

through it. I needed to escape from colleagues at lunch-time and just go and crumple up somewhere, relax and feel depressed (sounds weird, I know). The rest of the time I could generally make myself look alive and find ways to manage my feelings of distress without alerting others, and I knew I would be worse off at home. **Stephanie**

Debate continues about the benefits and downsides of the disclosure of a disability either at a job interview or, later, when in the job. Disclosure is unlikely to happen routinely. Applying for the job in the first place implies an assumption—that the job applicant considers themselves unimpaired in any way that would affect them in their job performance.

Disclosing, however, can create a more open climate where the employee doesn't have to hide their disability, the workplace may be able to provide some support, and any change in the employee's behaviour will be seen in a wider context than solely as a performance issue. It also enables quicker and more effective help if the person becomes ill while at work. Some views about disclosure are provided in Chapter 8.

6
Support
From the team and from the sidelines

' It's harder to pretend with colleagues. They see you day in and day out and can notice the wear and tear. I have started jobs when I am depressed, and people then think it's just you coming out of your shell when you emerge from depression. One of my friends said I was like a librarian when I first started. He couldn't believe how lively I became a few months later.

Most of the time my colleagues have not known I have bipolar disorder. You can get away with a lot. People are in their own worlds, with their own concerns. I'm pretty good at faking my way through it now. People have worked out that I am smart and question why I am doing such-and-such a job. That has been awkward when I haven't wanted to disclose my reasons.

When I have told colleagues, it has been great when they ask me lots of questions and really try to work it out. There are some common misunderstandings. Usually I get 'But you are such a happy person, you can't possibly get depressed.' I wish.

Once I bring colleagues up to speed with the nuances of the illness, they can be a real asset. In one job, I explained that when I am depressed it is hard to get motivated and I might forget to do things like wear makeup or earrings. We started joking about that by giving me a mark out of ten every day for effort. It kept me paying attention to the little things (and made me smile).

Another good thing about disclosing to a wide range of colleagues is that you end up hearing lots of stories about bipolar disorder or mental illness in general. In fact, you tend to become the 'office counsellor', referring others to the GP, etc. You end up knowing others in the organisation who have experienced mood disorders.

That's pretty amazing. When you talk openly, then others build up the confidence to do so as well.

In a practical sense, colleagues can double-check your work when you are worried about your concentration. They can let you off the hook from Friday night drinks. They don't mind if you are not full of ideas like you normally are. **Stephanie**

Colleagues at work may be the first to notice that someone has developed a mood disorder. Though it is a sensitive subject, it can be helpful if someone who is depressed understands that others are concerned for them. Hopefully, their immediate manager notices things like irregularities in their attendance, their impaired capacity to interact with others and contribute to a team, and a lag in the speed and accuracy in completing tasks. When the individual's mood starts to affect their work performance, it should be a signal for them to seek professional help or at least to discuss their physical symptoms with their general practitioner. Their depression may often be accompanied by disrupted sleep and diffuse aches and pains. As their mood state becomes more public, it is helpful to reinforce to them that the sooner they consult their doctor, the quicker and more effective their treatment will be.[1]

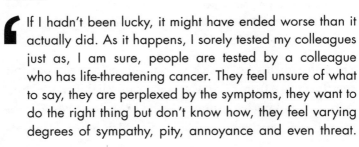

If I hadn't been lucky, it might have ended worse than it actually did. As it happens, I sorely tested my colleagues just as, I am sure, people are tested by a colleague who has life-threatening cancer. They feel unsure of what to say, they are perplexed by the symptoms, they want to do the right thing but don't know how, they feel varying degrees of sympathy, pity, annoyance and even threat.

But ultimately it was my colleagues who helped me in ways that others around me didn't. It was not studied, instructed help. It was instinctive, based on good hearts — the best kind of help. **Trish**

When you do suffer from any kind of mental illness in a work environment it is so important to work with a team. You will be amazed at the support you will receive as long as your colleagues see that their support is not just a one-way street and you are prepared to support them when they need help. **Natasha**

My advice is, find a support person in the workplace. I find someone I can trust and let him or her know about my condition and what it means. I ask them for 'reality checks'. **Shona**

Unbeknownst to me, work colleagues first started noticing my mood swings, increasing pessimism and seeming personality changes more than two years ago. Depression had crept up on me. **Richard**

For me, the most useful and successful strategy for lost insight into my condition is the appointment of 'minders'. These are people who see you frequently, either at work or home, and are able to observe your behaviour on a regular basis. **Marnie**

The consequences of a sick workmate include the possible overflow work from their absences or unreliability, the difficulties in working with someone who is 'low' or 'high', and the special provisions they may be given which other employees don't get—even though these others are hard-working and conscientious (and may even have trying circumstances outside of work that they are managing so that their work is not affected). Humanity, generosity and a healthy work environment encourage support of a workmate experiencing difficulty with depression or bipolar disorder. A manager or boss with some knowledge of mental health issues can cushion the impact of an employee's faltering performance at work. Also, understanding a few of the circumstances—while respecting an individual's privacy—can go some way towards others' acceptance of work performance that is temporarily impaired.

OBSERVING MENTAL ILLNESS IN A WORKMATE

Some of us had begun to voice our discontent to each other about our colleague's attendance, performance and mood. We were not aware of any personal problems or our workmate's depression, and indeed we began to behave in a distant way towards this employee, which no doubt contributed to his feelings of depression and isolation. Fortunately, our manager was a very understanding person who sought out the depressed employee and discussed work and personal issues with him, face to face, and in a non-threatening manner, something which did wonders for all of us. As a consequence of his speaking to our manager, a number of things happened in our workplace.

Firstly, the manager communicated to the rest of the staff that worked closely with him, with his permission, that our workmate had been experiencing depression, as well as some personal issues, which explained why his performance had dropped off considerably. This communication helped us all be more understanding and forgiving of our workmate's temporary drop in performance.

Secondly, the manager helped our workmate gain the psychological support he needed, by suggesting that he discuss his problems with his GP, who consequently referred him to a psychologist and also started him on a course of antidepressants.

Thirdly, our workmate was given reduced hours on a temporary basis, and access to personal leave, in order to give him the space to heal, and to resolve issues that had been affecting his performance at work. After a month of reduced hours and the right professional support, he returned to working full hours, and all the previous issues with his work performance and attendance have since reduced considerably.

This example was not given to suggest that all issues are magically solved by communicating personal problems to employers and colleagues, but to illustrate that from my experience, workmates and employers are more inclined to forgive tardiness, absenteeism, lower productivity and mood changes if they are aware of the contributing factors. The French proverb 'To understand all is to forgive all' indeed has some relevance in the workplace. Such understanding will not immediately resolve all the issues associated with depression in the workplace yet, from experience, it appears that such understanding leads employers and colleagues to give people space in which to heal. In this case, my manager was observant and understanding enough to actually initiate the communication and approach our workmate with depression, yet unfortunately not all managers are so inclined. This is where the depressed person has a role. One way of ensuring our employers and work colleagues know about depression is by telling them. **Vicki**

HARD LABOUR: A SNAPSHOT OF MOOD DISORDERS IN THE WORKPLACE

' Most often trying to work when you're depressed is like trying to scale Everest in sandals. Here, we get a glimpse of a day in the life of a depression sufferer (me), and the things that help and hinder ...

7.30 a.m.: I arrive at the office. I don't have to be here at this time; it's completely self-inflicted. But I am because I can't deal with peak-hour traffic. (The parking's really good at this hour of the day too.) The sun is still waking up so the air is cool. I let myself in the back door, climb the carpeted stairs, and switch on the lights and the central air-conditioning.

While my computer boots up, I go to the kitchenette, empty the dish rack and put away all the plates and coffee mugs. It's not because I'm an ultra-considerate employee; it's because doing this makes me feel like I've accomplished something before the day has even begun.

Today I am wearier than normal; my husband, who also suffers from depression, had a bad night, so we are both running on little sleep. I empty my little tub of muesli into a bowl, douse it with milk and bring it to my desk, and then munch on it as I scan through the pile of emails the internet dumps into my inbox. My mental list of things I need to do starts to loom large, so I exorcise it by making it an actual one. Some days this piece of paper is all that stands between me and total panic.

8 a.m.: I hear the back door open. My boss comes

trudging up the stairs. He waves at me as he enters his office. He looks the way I feel.

'How're you going?' he says, re-emerging and making a beeline for the coffee machine.

'Blecch.'

'Yeah, me too.'

My boss is the prince of bosses. He knows what it's like to live with depression, having shared quarters with it for more than twenty years. He and I both hold membership in the depressed spouses club. He shocked me once by encouraging me to nap on the job—if that was what I needed to do to get through the day: 'Just drag the beanbag into your office and shut the door for an hour. I've done it myself from time to time.' I've tried not to abuse the privilege but it's nice to know I have his permission. In fact, it never ceases to amaze me how much my employers will tolerate as long as I put in the hours and get the work done: I can saunter down the corridors in bedroom slippers, knit through meetings, absent myself from the office for several hours in the middle of the day for counselling sessions, and play and sing along to indie rock music at some volume (as long as the door is shut), and they wouldn't bat an eyelid. In terms of flexibility, they are contortionists.

8.30 a.m.: The rest of the staff straggle in. We are a small company—a baker's dozen of misfits all touched by the black dog in some way. The kitchenette fills with the sound of the kettle boiling, the toaster popping, coffee grains getting knocked into the bin, bang bang. Half of us keep bread in the freezer and butter in the fridge because we can't quite manage breakfast at home. I read somewhere that free breakfast offered by a number of

New York public schools had the favourable effect of boosting attendance and grades; sometimes I wonder what would happen if workplaces followed suit. Ah well, I suppose we can't all work for Google ...

9.30 a.m.: I've been here for two hours, but even so, the swing of things leaves me standing by the slippery dip. It's partly fatigue and partly the deadlines nipping at my heels. I open up another document and try to work, then realise I've read the same paragraph three times without my brain processing it into English. It's too easy to procrastinate with the playground of the internet at my fingertips. But that is not what they're paying me for.

10.30 a.m.: The diagnosis is the same as an hour ago: I'm stuck—sandbagged—jammed. I can't concentrate, but I need to; I can't make decisions, but they're crucial; I can't do anything, but it all needs to be done. Stress starts to rise like a crimson tide. Guilt starts pounding at my door. Anxiety starts sharpening its claws. This is not what they're paying me for ... There's nothing for it; I need a lifeline. I need to phone a friend. So I log on to instant messenger and, sure enough, they're there.

Clancy: Hey.

Chump Chop: Hello, how goes it?

Venting to them is fast-food therapy, but right now, I crave it. I crave their sympathetic ears, their lively keyboard patter, their genuine concern, lifting me up. I consume ten minutes of banter, my fists unclench, and I return like a recalcitrant child to the task at hand. My friends take up their stations in the background and stand like sentinels, witnessing me string together words, sentences, paragraphs, sections—the wheels slowly turn, momentum returning.

1 p.m.: Lunchtime. I'm behind and want to eat at my desk so I don't have to stop, but I have a standing date with Linda that propels me outside. (Hours of working under climate control causes me to forget its artificiality; in the real world, I recall my need for sun.) Once a week, we meet, rant and spill our guts—sometimes over dumplings, sometimes over bubble tea. We're fortunate our offices are close by. We're fortunate our bosses believe in rest and refreshment, and don't frown on us taking the full hour.

Today, Linda listens more than she speaks because I can't help rambling and I need to know she's felt the world from my shoes. I know I'm repeating myself; I'm glad she doesn't mind. I'm pathetically grateful for the time she gives me—grateful she still enjoys my company even though I'm like this.

2 p.m.: We have our weekly staff meeting in the boardroom. The finances are looking grim and the outlook grimmer. Sometimes I think it's only by the grace of God that our company stays afloat. We get along by blood, sweat and a fierce love for what we do. We like working here. Yes, even me—even when working feels like wading through treacle and I'd prefer instead to drown. 'I love my job, I love my job,' I whisper, echoing Emily Blunt in *The Devil Wears Prada*. 'I love my job ...'

3 p.m.: I'm down to the final hour of the day, but my grip is slipping. If I can, I save the mindless tasks for last as my brain is less active and much less awake than at 7.30 a.m. I look at my list—at all the uncrossed items, at how much there is to go. I calculate times and tasks as though I'm perambulating underwater. I'm only human; I can't do it all. It's time to look reality in the face and declare the day's officially coming to a close.

I save essential files to my USB drive, then shut down my computer. I say goodbye to my boss as I exit the floor. It helps that he trusts me. I have a good track record; he knows I'll get it done. It might be at three in the morning when I do it from home, but he won't care; that's what flexi-time is for, right?

In the car, I put the key in the ignition and say a prayer, thanking something larger than me: for the day and the things I've achieved, for my strength, for my friends, for my work. It's this—routine, regulations, relationships and the rhythm of activity—that gets me through and helps me function like a human being instead of a broken-down machine. Why else would I get out of bed in the morning? Why else would I leave the house to enter the world?

The engine starts. I throw the car into gear, spin the wheel, set my course for the road and beat the traffic home. **Connie**

It is natural to 'back off' rather than reach out to a colleague who is showing signs of depression, and fellow workers will often attribute changes to some temporary and external event. Tell-tale signs, however, lie in the global and out-of-character changes in behaviour (rather than, for instance, explicable and temporary irritability during end-of-year pressures). These include missed deadlines, unexplained absences, lateness, lack of energy, lack of focus, and irritability. This can provide an opening for fellow workers and managers to approach the individual—initially to see how they can help with tasks and projects that are faltering. Hopefully, in this setting the individual may let down his or her 'game face' so that it is possible to encourage them to seek professional help.

A good workplace environment is open enough that employees feel comfortable approaching workmates and managers and are also aware of resources available for support. In this environment, managers will have been equipped with the skills to approach an employee who is not managing—for any reason. Early approach helps earlier resolution, which, in turn, helps everyone. Explanations to others (with the affected individual's permission), fair reallocation of duties, efficient management of an employee's illness so that all have some expectations of the implications for schedules, and then staged return to work after treatment ensure the containment of any knock-on effects from the illness, be it physical or mental.

Return to work can be problematic if poorly managed. A recent report found that it is more difficult to reintegrate into the workforce during recovery from mental illness than from physical illness[2], because workmates and managers lack knowledge about mental illness and this can result in inadvertent lack of support and poor follow-up. In the study, successful return to the workplace was associated with some negotiation of shorter working hours, reduced tasks or workload, and communication between the employee, line manager and any occupational health assistance to plan an effective return-to-work package. Only a quarter of those experiencing depression were offered stress management advice, in spite of its known benefits. Additionally, organisations who made health services such as physiotherapy and cognitive behaviour therapy available to affected employees found that they returned to work at an earlier stage than those who were not offered such supports.

7
Individual fitness
Assisting recovery from impairment

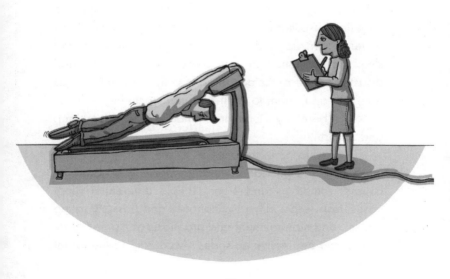

In the following excerpts, workers share their views about measures that could improve life at work. Such measures are not expensive to incorporate and help to create a climate in which the workforce becomes healthier and more productive. On the other hand, some individuals are out of step with their work environment and this mismatch can cause grief for both sides. The person may hide their impairment, or can't afford to recognise it, until the situation reaches crisis point because mental illness is too stigmatising to reveal.

> I was ashamed, embarrassed and very reluctant to see a psychiatrist, even when my doctor suggested that such a move might counter my burgeoning depression. I thought that to admit to having some sort of mental illness was to commit professional suicide. **Rick**

> What are the key topics in tackling mood disorders in the wider workplace? This bald list below is primarily for white-collar occupations. Further considerations would apply to specific blue-collar industries, whether long-distance truck drivers (poor diet and a lack of exercise, shift work and sleep deprivation, stimulant abuse), agriculture (natural disasters, toxic pesticides, market collapses), mining (its dangers, and boom to bust) and manufacturing (soulless factories beset by Durkheim's anomie and alienation), and so forth.
>
> First, *education*: this needs to be straightforward, interesting and provide up-to-date information about the causes, symptoms and signs, simple differential diagnoses, tests (especially physical ones and possibly rating scales), and management and prognosis of mania/hypomania and depressive episodes. According to the target

audience, reference could be made to 'mixed states', postnatal depression and puerperal psychosis, dysthymic disorder, cyclothymia, and mood phenomena associated for example with substance abuse, schizophrenia and possibly schizoaffective disorder, and the symptomatic depression induced for example by post-viral states, endocrine dysfunction, certain cancers, cardiac bypass surgery and medication side-effects.

The concepts of *primary*, *secondary* and *tertiary prevention* could be covered. Under primary prevention strategies are such factors as physical health, balanced diet, adequate exercise and sleep, avoidance of alcohol and drug abuse, cultivation of hobbies and interests, and the benefits of community involvement. This information could be conveyed orally and in written form by expert individuals and institutions, and a forum created for questions and answers that includes active audience participation. Falsehoods on the internet and elsewhere need to be dispelled as part of this.

Patently, this is a vast topic about which much more can be written. The workplace is a key area for the genesis, recognition and management of mood disorders, so that suffering, economic loss and community mishaps can be promptly and appreciably reduced. **Jake**

On the noticeboard here at work there are posters to raise awareness of coeliac disease, to offer free flu shots and to encourage staff to take up the offer of free healthy heart checks. I've never seen anything on that noticeboard about mental health issues. They say that approximately one in five individuals experiences mental illness at some point in their lives. This begs the question—how many employees in this very building are mentally ill? In my immediate team of fifteen people, at least three of my colleagues must have experienced a mental illness at some point in their lives. Yet I don't know and I will probably never know because we don't like to ask. I don't know if the real reason my colleague George was away for a week with the flu was because he was too depressed to come to work. Too often, I have felt the need to hide my real illness within the guise of a more respectable illness that everyone is bound to suffer from at some point in time; everyone can sympathise with the aches and pains of the flu but not everyone can relate to the profound despair that paralyses an individual suffering from depression. I'm counting on this sympathy to help me to get away with my absence; sympathy is inextricably linked to understanding, and experience tells me that our understanding of mood disorders within the workplace is poor.

I don't know what the solutions are and I probably don't have sufficient distance from my own experience yet to suggest many. But given that my own experience is all I really have to go on at this point, I would argue that we need to take initiatives in workplaces to encourage openness about mental health issues. We need to do things which are as simple as putting up posters on the wall and offering staff information on where they can get help if they need it. We need to remove the stigma of shame and secrecy and encourage honesty.

Personally, I'm hoping that in writing this I have taken that crucial first step on my journey towards honesty.
Karen

> As far as colleagues and companies understanding you—well, I must say that we are still a special breed to the uninformed, that is, most people. Until mood disorders are more clearly accepted by society we will remain a confusing group to the 'norm'. More and more people are accepting the reality of a broken mind but to the majority we, those who have been marked by mental illness, remain weak or strange. I urge you, the bearer of a mood disorder, to reject the 'snap out of it' mentality. You need to take a strong hold of yourself, rise above criticism and believe that you are not your illness, though it will bleed you from time to time.
>
> As I look back, I realise the company I worked for was probably willing to help me. Unfortunately, the illness caused such hypersensitivity that everything became distorted. I didn't have a name for my illness until this episode struck me down. Through seeing a psychiatrist and learning about what was wrong with me, I became equipped to shed the shame and put my boldness back on and find strategies that helped me to cope effectively.
> **Maria**

WORKPLACE PROGRAMS THAT SUPPORT MENTAL HEALTH AND RESILIENCE

When the culture in the workplace is sufficiently accepting that people in the organisation suffering from a mood disorder are able to admit to it, they can progress to the next step—seeking treatment. In an open environment it becomes less complex to define and sort through the problem, both for the employee and the organisation. An employee who was adept at his or her job can be restored to previous performance levels more readily if both sides can put their cards on the table.

Extended sick leave offered by, for instance, a sympathetic GP, but in the absence of more integrated management of a mood disorder, can be unhelpful. More employees are asking for sick leave certificates and doctors are issuing them for common musculoskeletal and mild to moderate mental health problems. Findings from an Australian study indicate that people on certified sick leave will 'commonly start down a slippery slope': after twelve weeks off work, their risk of becoming long-term unemployed rose dramatically, and six months of extended sick leave led to only a 20 per cent chance of that person still being in the workforce five years into the future. The problem is being replicated in the UK, the US and Canada too, according to this study.[1]

However, rather than extended absence from the workplace, the more effective solution is to seek organisational and therapeutic support to overcome an individual's lowered ability to cope in the workplace.

 When I told them I wasn't perfect, guess what? They told me about the bad things in their life. I even became close friends with another teacher suffering from depression too. After my breakdown, I started walking baby steps again. A rehabilitation program; not taking on too much of an overload; trying to say no more often; the right medication, therapy, etc.

So what happens to other people like me in the workplace who aren't so lucky? Or, rather, what should happen, so that we can reach out to each other and get help when the feelings of isolation, depression, anxiety and emotional paralysis overwhelm us?

We need to know about any employee assistance programs in advance. We need our manager/boss to recognise and ask about our symptoms in a confidential and caring manner. If that means workshopping with staff and experts about mood disorders, so be it. We don't want your diagnosis, but we do want your referral, understanding, kindness and flexibility. And above all we want you to listen to us. **Aisha**

' Recently it's been proved to my husband, John, and me that there are employers and organisations out there that take the wellbeing of their employees seriously. That includes employees who are dealing with mood disorders in their lives. When John's most recent employer found out he was ill, the employer responded by letting John know he understood, and offered him the space required for recovery. Without hesitation he made sure John knew that his work for them was greatly valued, and that he still had a future with the company. He was told that when he was ready, all he had to do was have the conversation with his employer about planning his transition back into the workplace.

My last employer was also amazing. When I told my CEO that John was ill and that there were immediate things I had to deal with, his response was, 'What can we do here at work to support you through this?' This blew me away. It was understood that I would need time off work to care for my husband, and this was dealt with in a most constructive way. It was all about my employer being part of a solution to help me do what I needed to do. I worked together with her in coming up with a temporary work plan that made sure I could care for John and look after myself. She helped me to reach a balance of maintaining some connection with work, while still enabling the flexibility I needed to get through this stressful period. I thought that this approach was so insightful and it helped me greatly. It was definitely a 'Hallelujah!' moment. This is what it should be like: out in the open, completely constructive, supportive and respectful.

These experiences highlight that effective management of mood disorders within the workplace relies on three things: first, the acceptance in the wider community that mental illness exists and is not much different to managing any other chronic illness. Second, that employers (and employees) are educated about mood disorders and other mental illnesses and, importantly, the signs of illness in their employees. Third, that bosses and management recognise that implementing supportive strategies not only helps in the recovery process, but also is a smarter choice in developing and retaining valuable employees.

In using a proactive approach, employers not only help to make the bleak times less stressful, but they have the opportunity to be an important part of people moving forward with their lives. If you feel valued, respected and secure, the fallout that beckons, the hopelessness, may just be that little less intense. It is the sum of small steps that finally has us up the mountain.
Cassie

WORKPLACE TRAINING AND SUPPORT

Workplace programs appropriate to the organisation/ industry when competently delivered to staff (including bosses and managers) can improve a work culture significantly. A program that presents positive strategies, such as ways to achieve efficiency and inoculate oneself against stress, has been found to encourage an employee to look more widely at ways of improving their own resilience and time management, and raise their awareness of a better work/life balance and a healthier lifestyle. Mental health education and dealing with impairment can be included in this. The effectiveness of such programs depends on the workplace 'match', and how genuinely such programs are embraced by senior management in the organisation.[2]

More industries are implementing employee and managerial resilience programs to foster good mental health—training that helps recognise workplace risk factors and ways of extending support. Employers and employees are taught how to recognise the signs and symptoms of mental illness, not in order to 'diagnose' such people but to refer them to professional help.

Canada has a history of innovative labour education programs, and one organisation estimated that it saved US$8 million in reduced absenteeism, and garnered higher productivity and better use of resources, from a US$4 million investment in employee wellbeing and a healthy workplace environment. Programs such as an onsite parent resource centre and extended benefits were welcomed, and absenteeism dropped by 60 per cent from the Canadian average; improved health and lower levels of substance abuse were also demonstrated.[3] Another example, from the UK, is an employee training course which involved a seven-week cognitive behavioural program that aimed to help employees evaluate and change any dysfunctional work-related thoughts, attitudes and behaviours. A follow-up of the outcome found improved employee job satisfaction and effectiveness, and decreased job turnover, and this was still the case two years later.[4]

BENEFITS OF OCCUPATIONAL HEALTH AND STAFF ASSISTANCE PROGRAMS

Organisations with trained occupational health staff can handle the sensitive issues around depression and bipolar episodes at work by advising and supporting the employer and the employee, negotiating any special provisions, and tracking leave entitlements and the timing of the return to part-time or full-time work. They are versed in the particular stresses of the work environment and can also coordinate with treatment providers, while respecting the employee's need for confidentiality.

An employee assistance program (EAP) is a work-based preventative and proactive program. Its functions include assessment, emergency intervention, substance abuse expertise, short-term counselling and referral services for employees, either in-house or contracted from an outside provider. It aims for early detection and resolution of work and personal problems. To be effective, however, it should be 'customised' to the organisation's needs, issues and culture.

The advantages of staff who have been trained in initial intervention in mental health issues is that they understand the parameters involved in structuring assistance for, and the expectations of, an individual with a mood disorder. These skills mean that, from the outset, both parties know what they can reasonably expect of each other. A staff member trained in the area can guide feedback from the employee, weigh up the employee's symptoms and their severity, witness the effectiveness of treatment, consider the likelihood of relapse (and identify and avoid issues that lead to relapses), and determine the level of mental acuity and stamina the job requires.

In-house mentoring or peer support is also helpful, and not solely for mental health problems.

Such programs can also manage the situation where an employee is ready to return to work yet wishes to postpone it, or the person who is over-eager to get back to work or attempts to return to a fuller schedule than is advised by the treating practitioner. Other aspects of this area to be managed include any reasonable accommodations needed by the employee to rejoin the workforce, the pace of their reintegration and its effect on their work (and their team).

Effective management is best focused on job performance. The employee can be given a job description to help them assess suitable work during reintegration into the workplace after recovery from a bout of mental illness. After all best efforts have been made by the organisation, if reintegration is not successful, the organisation is not expected to offer a different job or to create a new job for the employee.

8
Carrying an injury into the game
To disclose or not to disclose?

ummm...

‘ Increase the understanding of mood disorders among your coworkers by demonstrating how well you work. When you know the time is right, disclose your condition. Ideally, management should know too, but unfortunately a disclosure at this level may impact negatively on your career. This is a good time to talk to the coaching staff— your support team. Sadly, I have had to creatively hide the gaps in my résumé in order to find work, but I am determined not to do that again. **Stuart**

There is continuing debate about whether to disclose previous episodes of depression or bipolar disorder when either applying for a job or while in the position. The following accounts canvass the issue. First, here are some thoughts from a woman managing her career and bipolar disorder. Her disorder emerged suddenly and acutely and for the first time when she was 27 years old, remitted, and then returned when she was 34, when she had five episodes over two and a half years. She is now stable, thanks to skilful self-management and the help of health professionals, together with the correct combination of medications.

TO DISCLOSE OR NOT TO DISCLOSE?

‘ Wellness strategies (treatments, lifestyle, social support, etc.) may help people manage episodes without necessarily alerting their workplace that they have a mood disorder. Anyone can be ‘off their game’ for a stretch for a number of reasons (a marriage break-up, studying for exams, a new baby…). If the person, their family and health professionals can bring things under control, is there any need to disclose at work? Perhaps this will turn out to be an isolated episode? What is the risk of being perceived differently? Many people will choose to manage their mood disorder without disclosing, or disclose in a very limited way (perhaps to human resources staff or to their line manager). Clients and colleagues may not even be aware that someone has lost their 'sparkle' or that they are a little 'wired'.

The 'little white lie'. The first fib you need is the one to cover the gap on your CV. Mine says that for the second half of 1998 I was travelling. Well, yes, I certainly did travel. The itinerary was SYD–NYC–LON–psychiatric hospital–parents' house. Quite a trip!

Then you need one for the recruiter who looks at your CV (which has your degrees and investment banking experience) and asks you why you want a significantly lower level position. This was before downshifting/sizing was fashionable, but I said that I wanted to get out of the rat race, that I'd been OVERSEAS (as per lie no. 1 above) and now I could see that the long hours/pressured path was not for me. In the end, I found that the best way to deal with this issue was to do temporary work, because it doesn't matter how senior you are for that, and no one talks to the temps anyway.

There are a few other assorted half-truths that come in handy. For example, when you are in a new position, people may want to promote you or wonder why a 'smart girl like you' is doing a job like this. It thus becomes easier not to mention your illustrious past and perhaps to temporarily dumb down your résumé. If workmates are hassling you every Friday night to come for a drink, it might be helpful to invent a clingy boyfriend/girlfriend/spouse who expects you to come straight home.

I think we have to be a little economical with the truth. You need time to absorb the situation and decide how much information you want to disclose. Although community knowledge about mood disorders has improved since I was diagnosed, there is still a long way to go. I still would never disclose in a job interview. I would also never disclose prior to serving my probation period.

Additionally, that privacy helped me regain my sense of self. I didn't have to worry about what others thought of bipolar disorder. I didn't have to work out how to explain it. I didn't know if it was even going to happen again.

The downside to that strategy is that I felt inhibited in forming social relationships with work colleagues because I couldn't explain a large part of my life to them. I wouldn't go to work drinks because I was worried I would have a few glasses of wine and then disclose more than I had planned to.

By not disclosing you are missing out on accommodations that an employer might be able to make for you. If your work is slipping, an employer will treat it like a performance issue rather than a health issue. However, by disclosing you also risk being adversely affected. Your employer may not handle the situation well. People might make assumptions that you are 'delicate' or not up to the demands of the job. Workplaces are political environments and your disclosure could be used against you. People might attribute things to your illness that are not reasonable. For example, if there is conflict involving the person with a mood disorder, people might assume it is caused by the mood disorder, rather than any of the normal range of problems that can occur in a workplace.

When I have disclosed in a workplace, I have found it best just to disclose to my line manager and/or HR. They should know they have to act responsibly and that there are legal obligations. They should ask your permission if they want to tell anyone else. When I did disclose in this way, I was able to arrange time off to see my specialist regularly while I was going on lithium. The absolutely best response was when a manager turned around and said, 'I have some understanding of the issues, my mother has schizophrenia.' That was just wonderful—we were already on the same page.

I needed managers to know that when I am depressed, my work will probably still be of a normal standard, but my mood will be much lower. I didn't want that to be misinterpreted as lack of interest or a bad attitude. It took me a long time though to be prepared to disclose like this. You need to feel confident that you can explain the illness and describe its impact on your work and what assistance you need. That takes time. You also need to feel confident that you could be assertive if something does go wrong. That's hard, especially if you are experiencing depression. Again, that's something I wouldn't have been able to consider in the early years of my illness.

I think when you disclose bipolar disorder, whether to a colleague or to a manager, you need to be prepared to explain it. People generally don't know much about it. Being elevated or depressed is not really an ideal time to be trying to do this. That makes disclosure a real challenge, too.

There was one environment where I was completely open about my illness. I didn't need time off and my work standard was fine; however, my life was difficult, day after day with depression. It helped that my managers and colleagues knew. I could just relax and be myself. It was easier for me to make friends in that environment because I didn't have any secrets. I could even go to Friday night drinks. There were still risks with this decision and I only did it in an environment where I was not looking to get promoted. I wouldn't have been prepared to disclose had that been the case. **Stephanie**

REASONS FOR/AGAINST DISCLOSURE OF DEPRESSION OR BIPOLAR DISORDER

The following information is excerpted from a very comprehensive document covering disclosure issues: *Choosing Your Path: Disclosure, it's a personal issue.*[1] For rights, responsibilities and legislation that are relevant to your own situation, consult information about the obligations of employers to employees and employees to employers provided by your own state, province or country.

Why a person may choose not to disclose when applying for, or employed in, a job

- They judge that they can manage their job without additional support.
- They have put in place adequate structures to ensure that any impairment does not impede their job.
- They may feel that they would be treated differently, perceived in a negative or discriminatory way.
- Their mood disorder may be in remission and therefore not considered relevant.

The downsides of employee non-disclosure

- They lose the chance to negotiate work-related adjustments, especially in a crisis.
- They risk any impact of the mood disorder on the job being treated as poor work performance.
- They can't use their position to assist in raising the awareness and support of employment of people with mood disorders.
- If the mood disorder could reasonably be seen to cause a health and safety risk for other people in the workplace, failing to disclose that risk could be a breach of an employee's obligations.

Why a person may disclose a previously undisclosed mood disorder

Every employee's situation can change and such changes can impact on the previous decision not to disclose. Such changes include:

- increased workloads that might impact on mental health
- illness that is a direct consequence of work stresses
- career developments (new work location, new manager, new colleagues)
- a greater understanding of organisational policies and procedures
- finding that their disability does, in fact, impact on their daily activities, and vice versa
- understanding the relevance of their disability to a particular situation; for instance, they may find aspects of their disability are of benefit in their job—such as in welfare work

- changes to their personal situation
- developing a new episode of serious illness that requires support and work-related adjustments (such as time off work, lighter duties, change to work hours or equipment)
- feeling more secure and comfortable in the job, and finding that disclosure will not lead to discriminatory attitudes and actions
- the need to implement work-related adjustments to ensure a healthier environment
- in the instance of disciplinary meetings due to poor work performance related to the impairment of a mood disorder, disclosure may be required to inform management so that they may develop work-related adjustments, rather than implementing poor work performance procedures.

If disclosing a mood disorder, what to disclose and to whom?

Employees need to prepare how they would like to disclose their mood disorder. Information presented should be relevant to the job but doesn't have to be in-depth medical or personal information. It is important to identify the right person to disclose to: employer, supervisor, human resources department, support services such as equal employment opportunity units, equity/social justice unity or employee support staff, if these exist. External supports such as union organisations, mental health programs, friends and/or work colleagues may also assist in formulating a plan prior to disclosing a disability.

The information presented to the appropriate person may include what the diagnosis is, why the employee has chosen to disclose it, how it impacts on performance at work, and the type of work-related adjustments that could assist.

Rights and responsibilities in disclosing a mood disorder when in the job

Employees have a right to:

- have information about their diagnosis treated confidentially and with respect; know what happens to this information; and have this information used only for implementing work-related adjustments and assessment of whether the inherent requirements of the position can be met
- respond to the questions that are relevant for identifying work-related adjustments.

Employees have a responsibility to:

- obtain assistance in identifying suggested work-related adjustments that might enable them to retain their position
- recognise that disclosure at the point of crisis may mean that work-related adjustments cannot be easily or successfully implemented
- disclose a mood disorder if the impairment is impacting on work performance and/or on the health and safety aspects of the work environment.

Employers have a right to:

- meet with the employee to discuss the issues and available supports in the organisation

- discuss with the employee the type of work-related adjustments that may be required for the job, and identify appropriate adjustments, timelines for implementing them, and times for follow-up
- organise feasible work-related adjustments.

Employers have a responsibility to:

- follow the standards set by any relevant legislation in relation to collecting, using and disclosing personal information
- follow the standards set by any relevant legislation so as not to discriminate by less favourable treatment; make reasonable workplace adjustments; and prevent workplace harassment
- assess any potential occupational health and safety implications
- assess the employee's request for work-related adjustments before making a claim of 'unjustifiable hardship'.

If an employer becomes aware that poor work performance is attributed to an employee's previously undisclosed mood disorder, the employer should:

- stop any disciplinary process
- address the disability issues and identify any work-related adjustments to assist the employee to meet the inherent requirements of the position
- provide a timeline for implementing the work-related adjustments
- if poor work performance continues after the identified timeline, recommence the disciplinary process with the employee.

DISCLOSURE—WHAT NEXT?

The following account is from a woman who, like most people with a mood disorder of any severity, prefers to disclose, depending on the work environment. It seems that most people who suffer from depression or bipolar disorder are not interested in the extra strain implicit in taking on the role as a sort of 'live poster' to advance destigmatisation, but if there is a supportive work environment it can be a relief to disclose—depending on how sensitively colleagues and supervisors handle the issue.

 THE DOWNSIDE OF MY 'GAME FACE'

I have been using the game face ever since I entered Wonderland (my recurring bipolar disorder). For many years I have employed this technique to get me through cyclical bad patches and in that time I have made good friends and achieved academically. I suspect game face comes instinctively to people with bipolar disorder because secrecy is a major drive when you have this condition—my instinct is to 'conceal at all costs'.

However, concealment has a downside. Maintaining the game face takes energy and the more depressed you are, the more energy you burn when projecting it. I find myself retreating from social contact when I reach this phase; however, work still has to happen. The end result is that I move into 'wipe-out mode' at home. In this mode, I am left with little to no energy to conceal the true nature of my internal landscape. Sadly, it is those nearest and dearest to me who get to live with this. I am lucky to have a wonderful nurturing family for this period.

Transparency—the rub

A nurturing environment leads me nicely to the other navigational tool I use in Wonderland. Transparency is a delicate issue. As with most things bipolar, it can be double-edged. Telling people about your condition can foster understanding and awareness and, in an environment of acceptance and tolerance, it becomes easier to manage bipolar swings. Obviously, you only tell people who you trust deeply. The entire planet doesn't need to know. Most of the time this form of openness works for me, but 'mid-meltdown' I confess I find my transparency intensely painful. I do not enjoy people getting to see me fall apart (after all, I have been vigorously hiding these moments for decades). So this is the rub. As with game face, transparency is a useful tool but it can be a two-sided blade and needs to be wielded carefully. Your ego must be prepared to let people see that you are not perfect. Ouch!

I have been very lucky. My mood disorder is not extreme and my workplace and family life is happy and supportive. I receive excellent therapy and have found truth in Nietzsche's observation: 'That which does not kill us, makes us stronger.' **Talia**

There is an unfortunate contradiction that resides in whether to disclose or conceal a mood disorder. The affected individual is unlikely to disclose because of the risk of discrimination and also their reasoning that their mood disorder is under control and is not impacting on their job performance. This means that the early intervention and support that the organisation could offer is not brought into play and crisis intervention becomes more likely—and crisis intervention can bruise everyone. It is also distinctly less effective for quick and successful medical and organisational management of the by now full-blown depressive or bipolar episode.

9
Agreeing on the goals
Aligning worker and workplace expectations

❛ Depression doesn't define who you are. You are a person coping with an illness. **Justin**

Here are employees' views about some possible adjustments—on both sides—to make it easier to accommodate diversity in the workplace. On the organisation's side, there are some general suggestions that can temporarily ease the load for a valuable employee who has been incapacitated with a depressive or hypomanic episode. These include:

* **restructuring the job**—for instance, temporarily cutting back on minor job duties and assigning 'fill-in' duties to another employee, with that latter employee being cut some slack elsewhere
* **flexible scheduling**—changing the start or end of the workday to accommodate side-effects of medication, scheduling in flexi-time for medical/psychological support appointments, allowing specific breaks during the workday, offering part-time work
* **flexible leave**—supporting the use of sick leave for mental health reasons or extending leave without pay over a hospitalisation or for time off
* **supportive modifications to the work environment**— as discussed with the affected individual; these might range from allocating a quieter room for them through to supplying a non-fluorescent desk lamp
* **providing a mentor**—a colleague or manager who is on the individual's wavelength who can assist the worker, maybe structuring the day's work with them at the outset and then checking in on how things are going during the day

- **changes in training**—allowing extra time and aids to learn job tasks.[1]

ACCOMMODATING DIVERSITY IN THE WORKPLACE

Alison has a full-time job and is also raising two young children. She has a depressive disorder that is manageable but she needs to structure her work carefully to prevent relapses. She is a valued employee and her job is a good fit with her abilities but she strives to keep her work to a steady flow and avoid becoming jostled and stressed. Here are her thoughts.

Imagine if workplace diversity existed; I mean truly existed in our society. Imagine if it was an invaluable tool used to increase productivity, improve morale and achieve the greatest outcomes. Imagine if employers recognised that effective deployment of diversity was a means by which empires could grow and thrive. Imagine if difference was no longer measured in terms of deviation from perfection. How much more we could create, how high our aspirations and how successful our communities would be ...

Are people with mood disorders recognised as individuals with diverse gifts and skills? Do employers make the most of the manic energy of the bipolar employee, use the sensitivity of the depressive to read people and situations, take advantage of the meticulous attention to detail of the obsessive compulsive? Do employers respect the need for individuals with mood disorders to have some 'down time' once in a while to regroup and recentre? Do they maximise the opportunity presented by such diversity in their industry or sector?

And on the other side of the coin, as individuals who suffer from mood disorders, do we attend therapy and medicate ourselves to gain tools to achieve happiness and success? Or do we try to discard a part of ourselves that we are ashamed of? Do we berate ourselves for our difference? Do we push ourselves to the end of our physical, emotional and spiritual tethers, refusing to ask for help until we have crashed through the safety rail and begun to slide down, down, into the gaping chasm of fear, anxiety and self-loathing that is always there, always waiting . . .

Throughout history, mood disorders have featured as part of the human condition—nervous disorders, melancholia, behavioural problems, 'the little girl with the curl'. Today these conditions have medical names—bipolar disorder, depression, OCD, ADHD—and we are bombarded with medical 'solutions', descriptions, prescriptions and potions. Our mood disorders are recognised as genuine conditions by the medical profession—like asthma or diabetes. Yet still it seems mental illness is a dirty secret, a weakness that is acceptable only if it is someone else's affliction. So we stumble along our confused path asking for help or not, looking for answers, or continuing to lose ourselves in endless questions, seeking support, or struggling on in our loneliness and isolation.

Perhaps it is time we took a stand and began to educate our communities and our workplaces; told the truth about living with mood disorders. Maybe it is our collective responsibility to unashamedly tell our stories. Why should mental illness make us victims? Why do we perpetuate our victim status by continuing to allow ourselves to be weighed and measured and found wanting by employers, colleagues and perhaps, most of all, by ourselves?

We do not understand our condition, so how can we expect others to accommodate our needs intuitively? Happiness, contentment, success, self-acceptance—these are not grand and unattainable goals. Collectively we have the capacity to move mountains. Despite our condition, we have unique gifts and strengths that should be recognised and nurtured.

When we come across someone who is blind or deaf, we find that their other senses are far more acute than those who have not lost a sense. How strong are the compensating limbs of the amputee? The person with a mood disorder may at times be paralysed with anxiety and fear, may be overly emotional, moody, angry or aggressive. But all have corresponding gifts and skills; strengths we should encourage and protect. With the right support from our colleagues and managers, they could bring out the best in us. With some self-acceptance— cutting ourselves some slack once in a while—we could bring out the best in ourselves.

Employers are responsible for implementing fair and equal employment opportunities, for introducing workplace diversity policies, for supporting their staff to maximise productivity. But standing up for ourselves, respecting ourselves and asking the world to take us as we are, to give us the space to use our creative talents and find ways to manage our problems—asking for acceptance and respect—for that, *we* are responsible. **Alison**

There is a postscript to the excerpt immediately above: this is the story mentioned in the Introduction to this book. Alison had resigned from job number two during an episode of depression when she had felt that she wasn't able to manage it alongside her commitment to her family. The employer she had worked for before job number two chanced across her story (it won a prize in the Black Dog Institute's writing competition) and was impressed with her observations: they offered Alison her former job back but with more family-friendly working hours.

WHAT DO WORKERS WANT? AND WHEN DO THEY WANT IT?

The old saying still applies: 'If you want someone to do a good job, give them a good job to do.' Sometimes job quality can be markedly improved via quite simple adjustments. A level of unnecessary complexity is added when workers and management 'mind read' rather than communicate their needs clearly to each other—or the organisation's culture may discourage frank communication. The following table illustrates that employers and employees are not always on the same wavelength.

An informal ranking of the same list by employers and by employees[2]

	What the boss thinks the employee wants	What the employee wants
1	Help with personal problems	Interesting work (and training for it)
2	Interesting work	Full appreciation of work done
3	High wages	A feeling of being involved in things
4	Job security	Job security

5	Personal loyalty of supervisor	High wages
6	Tactful discipline	Promotion and growth in the company
7	Full appreciation of work done	Good working conditions
8	A feeling of being involved in things	Personal loyalty of supervisor
9	Good working conditions	Help with personal problems
10	Promotion and growth in the company	Tactful discipline

Other workers surveyed[3,4] felt that their workplace could be improved by measures such as:

- reduced personal conflicts on the job
- training of managers and employees about how to resolve conflicts
- treating employees fairly and defining job expectations clearly
- giving employees adequate control over how they do their work
- allowing employees input into decision-making, explaining company policies, and employers talking openly with them
- ensuring adequate staffing and budgets to prevent work overload
- giving employees fair pay, not necessarily high pay
- offering support and rewarding employees' efforts
- encouraging cooperation, not competition
- providing human resources programs that are family-friendly

- providing flexible hours where possible
- reducing the amount of red tape
- providing an employee assistance program, an employee wellness program and a work/life balance program.
  Most sought some sort of employee organisation to represent their views.[5]

Job satisfaction is not specifically related to the employee's assigned task. Instead it is reliably related to 'organisational citizenship', which is defined as helping others and the organisation, and to the absence of bad citizenship (such as stealing from the employer).[6]

The following accounts cover some steps used by people to manage a successful return to the workplace, and strategies that they have found useful for remaining well and adapting to their mood disorder.

A STAGED RETURN TO WORK FOR AN EMPLOYEE IN RECOVERY

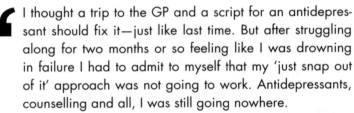

I thought a trip to the GP and a script for an antidepressant should fix it—just like last time. But after struggling along for two months or so feeling like I was drowning in failure I had to admit to myself that my 'just snap out of it' approach was not going to work. Antidepressants, counselling and all, I was still going nowhere.

Fortunately, my workplace has an employee assistance program which allows staff to access several confidential counselling sessions and I had a very supportive supervisor who allowed me flexibility in working hours. However, to my frustration, nothing worked, my anxiety heightened and my life seemed to be drifting. I started having panic attacks at the thought of going to work and even walking through the building to my office. I got to the point that I didn't want to drive anywhere near work, I avoided the shopping centre in case I ran into anyone I knew, and I hid inside my house in case people from work saw me in the yard.

Now, four months into recovery, I am back working part-time as part of an ongoing plan to get back into full-time work. So, what worked? In spite of my best efforts I am yet to find the magic pill or fairytale cure. Trying to work while I had depression, for me, meant that I actually had to take some time off. Changing to part-time work wasn't enough, I needed a break—time where I wasn't thinking and worrying and stressing about what was happening in the office and could concentrate on *me* for a while.

Look into what is available through your workplace's human resources/health and safety unit. My rehabilitation officer, for instance, has been a godsend—handling details like leave and payroll issues, and liaising between me and my supervisors when I was unable to cope even with calling in to let someone know I would not be at work that day. Even when I was on three months' leave, she would periodically give me a call, just to see how things were going and if there was anything she could do to help.

Not working brings its own stress. I went from full-time wages to unemployment benefits (having exhausted all my paid leave and savings long before), so now I had to worry about money. If you are eligible, make sure your doctor establishes a mental health care plan. For example, in Australia you can get money back from Medicare for psychologist visits under this plan. I would not have been able to keep going to mine without the reduced cost.

My psychologist encouraged me to seek expert help with my medication when it was becoming clear that what I was taking was not working for me this time. It took me several days to work up the courage to call my local mental health unit. At the time I was so ashamed of what I had let myself become, the thought of seeing a psychiatrist felt like yet another failure. My doctor from the acute care team was great: during the appointment he continued to reiterate the message that everyone was telling me—depression is something you can overcome, a medical condition as real as a broken leg or diabetes—but this time the message started to sink in.

Over the next few weeks I progressively changed medication and very slowly I started to feel better about things. Although the medication worked, it still took time for me to develop coping mechanisms and techniques to get back to work. I have only been back at work part-time and on a regular basis for two months, and in that time I have had my fair share of glitches.

When you have to push yourself every single day, consciously 'forcing yourself' to go to work, it is easy to derail. My return to work started with short visits or drop-ins for morning tea. My advice to others is—don't rush it. When you are broke and Christmas is just around the corner, it is impossible to not want to just get over it and get back to earning an income. Of course the first time something happened that I couldn't deal with, I fell back into my cocoon. It seemed easier to stay in bed and ignore the world.

To quote Winston Churchill, 'If you are going through hell, keep going.' This has become my slogan—and it does get easier. There are people who can help you. You don't need to share your innermost thoughts with the water-cooler people. Find out if your workplace has programs and don't be afraid to take advantage of them. If you are taking medication but not seeing and feeling any improvement, it might be time for a change.

My final bit of advice—give people a chance, they might surprise you. I felt humiliated and embarrassed dealing with something like anxiety and depression in front of peers and casual acquaintances at work, but it really is more common than you think. My first few days back, I felt like a bug under a microscope, and to be honest, my supervisor is still very sensitive to changes in my routine or mood, but depression is something more and more people are becoming aware of. Now that I can think about it more rationally, I know that this illness does not signal the end of future career prospects or that I am wearing flashing neon signs singling me out as the only person to have ever gone through something like this. **Jill**

HOW TO GET WELL AND KEEP WELL IN THE WORKPLACE

I have bipolar-schizoaffective disorder. I like to call it the rubbish bin of mental illness as it has a little bit of everything in it. For ten years I have lived with this and am proud to say I am seven years hospital-free.

Over this decade I have developed many strategies to tackle my mood disorder in the workplace. I found there is more to recovery and wellness than being a good girl and taking my medication to be socially acceptable. Some days looking after myself is a full-time job, so these are my 'Twelve Commandments':

1. I work part-time.
2. Shift work is out—my sleep must come first.
3. I take my annual leave—there is no need to work until you fall apart.
4. I 'chill out' during the day—12 noon is my lunchtime, and I leave the building.
5. I take sick leave when needed—sick leave is not just for when you're feeling nauseous or fluey.
6. I find a support person in the workplace and I ask them for 'reality checks' when I get too paranoid, when my anger is churning after a confrontation, or when I get stuck on a topic or overinvolved in personalities and office politics.
7. I bring my creativity to work. I write poetry and this is better than any diary I could keep. I make poems for people when they leave or for special occasions.
8. I set boundaries on my workload—yes, I will help others out but after I have attended to my own work first. I will take on extra duties provided they fit in with my workload. If it is too much, I let the boss know and I stop. I limit the number of tasks I volunteer for and stay away from evening and weekend work. That's *my* free time.
9. I get a good night's sleep—not sleeping can trigger an episode for me, or at least trigger anxiety about having one. If something is churning around in my brain at night, and I have had a previous bad night, I take something to help me to sleep.
10. I have a back-up plan. I have been with my current organisation for five years; I have five months worth of long service and sick leave up my sleeve; I live in a house with super-cheap rent. So even if I do get

sick one day, I can still support myself while I recover, without losing my job.

11. I've learnt to be patient—change has to happen sometime. Not everyone in the workplace has a positive or empathetic view of those with mood disorders, though I cringe when I hear other workers describe a client as 'nuts' or 'psycho'.

12. I decided long ago that you cannot change anyone's opinion and that I did not want to be the 'poster child' for mental illness within my current workplace. I have experienced discrimination and misunderstanding in the past, and been described as 'that one who went crazy a few years back and was never the same again'. Well, nobody could go through what those with a mood disorder have gone through and *not* be affected by it, which is why I put so much effort into keeping things in order. Though we may not stand up and shout and declare ourselves, we may be your workmates, your admin assistants and your managers. **Shona**

One trap I've constantly fallen into in the past is that sticky pot called perfectionism: 'I am fatally flawed therefore I must appear to be perfect.' Nothing struck terror into my heart more than thinking that someone might find out there was something wrong with me! Thus, no task was too arduous, no workload too great. And as these tasks were accomplished, colleagues would nod approvingly and pile more on my plate. A critical mass would occur, a point at which anyone would crack, and I'd come tumbling down. This would inevitably be followed by a tearful confession to my superiors and a divulgence of that greatest of sordid secrets: 'I suffer from depression.'

The moral of this particular story is simple: strive to be the best you can be, but realise that, like everyone else, you have limitations. You don't have to be superhuman. On reflection I've often found that the times when I nearly 'lost it' at work were times when *most* people would have been suffering great stress. I now find it useful to take a step to one side and analyse the situation. Is this a situation that most people would find stressful? What steps can I take to minimise my stress and get the job done? This rational path takes the self-flagellation factor out of play and allows me to move forward rather than getting stuck in a loop. **Briony**

I now work from home; my boss is fair and generous and has taught me a lot. He is the first work colleague with whom I have discussed my illness, and his reaction was one of empathy. **Mike**

Having 'hours to suit' me is a great aspect of the employment package. Mostly I will want the same regular hours, as a daily routine helps me manage my depression. But during more turbulent times of illness, this will still allow me to come into work, just later in the day. With depression, often it improves as the day goes on. **Suzette**

As these accounts clearly show, if both the organisation and the employee are able to play fair with each other, then there is a much higher chance of disclosure of the condition and successful resolution of any problems it is causing in the workplace. Depression or bipolar disorder, if left to run without intervention, can cause chronic problems, additional to those difficulties that are symptomatic of the disorders themselves—distortions in the individual's perceptions and lack of or overabundance of energy. Recognition of early warning signs of a recurrence—via the individual's improved self-management, hopefully generated by earlier disclosure of the condition and assisted perhaps by the 'outside insight' that a trusted other (family, friend, manager) can offer—is a start. Then, a transition to a template that the organisation has in place that clearly outlines support, rights and responsibilities, and results in a timeline for recovery and reintegration, can tackle a mood disorder in the workplace before it spoils that individual's chances and robs the organisation of a productive worker.

10
Improving the odds
Matching personal skills to the
workplace

' On the plus side, depression forced me to confront what was difficult at work. I couldn't continue the way things were. I didn't talk directly about my depression with my boss but I did tell him I needed more consistency and less responsibility. Being honest about what I needed to feel okay at work, rather than waiting until I felt completely overwhelmed, gave me the time out I desperately needed. Focusing on what I wanted from the workplace rather than apologising for my inability to cope with the status quo meant I didn't have to expose my vulnerability to my boss or my workmates, which I wasn't ready to do. **Helen**

' Then the depression kicked in. Living in London, one of the most expensive cities in the world, at the bleakest time of the year, I started looking for work. I no longer wanted to be a lawyer. I wanted to be a journalist. But legal work was all I was qualified to do. I came back home, my tail squarely between my legs, with no money, no job, and no hope.

Those days were some of the worst of my life. I couldn't listen to music. I couldn't watch television. I couldn't read. I couldn't do anything. I didn't want to get up in the morning, and when I did, I'd lie on the couch and stare at the ceiling. I couldn't think. I simply didn't want to exist anymore. There was absolutely no way I could work, let alone find employment.

So I started slowly. My first job was marking maths papers at a local tutoring school for four hours a week. I was earning five dollars an hour, but when I got that first pay packet it felt like a million dollars. Then I moved on to office temping work. The medication had kicked in by then, and I started getting bored doing menial office work. I needed bigger and better things to occupy my mind. I was actually thinking!

I stayed in that job a couple of weeks, and then got my break. A two-month contract in a government agency, writing policy, which ended up lasting nine months. Then, and only then, could I contemplate what had previously seemed so insurmountable, the task of completely changing my career.

Six years later I have done it. I succeeded. I beat this thing. **Jax**

There are some gentler ways to retransition to work before actually tackling the workplace again. Local councils and not-for-profit groups have part-time and transitional work opportunities in areas that are very beneficial to the community. Such involvements may be unpaid but satisfying, helping people in need, and providing structure and a transition to longer engagement in the workforce. The involvement is something for the CV and perhaps some useful connections will be made. Some examples, listed in a survey of 150 local governments' areas of 'unmet need', included jobs filling gaps in the provision of public and community transport, teachers' aides, home care support for the elderly and disabled, assistance in residential aged care, supporting people in crisis accommodation and domestic violence refuges, minor roadways repairs, community gardening, constructing and tending to bike paths, environmental schemes involving park clean-ups and regeneration schemes, general community services in education, child care and health care assistance, and volunteering in a variety of opportunities generated by work subsidies to private enterprises that then create jobs.[1]

The following account by Rubin demonstrates the strain that affects both the individual and the organisation when the job is not in line with personal values—especially as depression progressively affected his perceptions and energy. It is ironic that Rubin's job was to match people to positions. The second account, by Stuart, underlines that adjusting and fitting in to the workforce requires positive effort on the part of the individual, and in it Stuart outlines his game plan.

I was a recruitment consultant working for a major international industry player. On a daily basis the human heart was my concern and I desperately tried to put people into the right job. However, what began as a passion ended in an inner war where the real game was to sell people and the prize was a big commission.

I became known as the company sook. My boss would call me in and ask if I was okay but in my mind she hated me, so I wasn't going to share my personal feelings with her. All she wanted was for me to make money. More and more I was under the gun, being watched and questioned why I had gone from number one to the lowest performer. It didn't make sense to anyone—and least of all to me.

To survive it became necessary to leave this job. Getting out of bed took an extraordinary amount of strength, so further work was out of the question. I left the company and left behind my reputation of being 'the sook' and a 'corporate enemy'. I was even marched off the premises and not allowed to farewell anyone. Of course this was due to the negativity I was casting out upon my colleagues about the ridiculous notion that we cared for people. Human resources! You have got to be kidding, I thought. We sold human beings to work for people so our company could make money.

Slowly I made my way back to being myself again. Eight months in fact! It took so much courage that I can't even put it into words. What that episode did to me changed my life forever. It's now ten years on and I have experienced recurrent depressive episodes with similar severity. I now accept that it is a part of me, but there are things I can do to lessen the blow.

If you have a mood disorder and you are in a job that is too stressful or not in line with your own beliefs, then getting out is a form of self-protection. Life for 'us' needs to be simplified and appreciated from a different perspective. Make that perspective as uncomplicated as you can. Work is just part of your story—not your life. **Rubin**

STAYING IN THE GAME

Working with a mood disorder is sometimes like being a professional footballer. If you are like me you have trained hard for a long time and have endeavoured to reach optimum levels of fitness by attending special clinics and even taking daily supplements to achieve excellence. You are in the game because you enjoy it and because it pays the bills and you like being part of a team. Defence has become the cornerstone of your game and over time your tackle count has been well above the average. You possess fine attacking skills too, sometimes brilliant and creative they say, but because you put yourself out there you are prone to taking too many king hits—high tackles, late tackles, unexpected shoulder charges. But you keep getting up and rejoining the game even if you have been sidelined with injury for weeks, months, sometimes a full season.

But footballers only have ten or so years in the game—when you work with a mood disorder you are in it for life. That's a lot of tackling! So you need a game plan.

To begin, remember that injury often comes early in your career—you may even have shown a predisposition to injury before gaining selection. My career is a good example. What I saw as weakness, a failing, a lack of ability during my last year of tertiary study and my first year of teaching was in fact a serious depressive mood swing. What I felt midway through my second year of teaching—the energy, confidence, certainty and lack of judgement that culminated in me chasing the maths head teacher around the playground with a fire extinguisher before tendering my resignation—was in fact my first episode of hypomania. It is difficult to tackle a mood disorder in the workplace if you don't know or can't recognise that you have one. It is difficult to remain in the workplace at all!

Training too hard without appropriate rest can lead to major stress fractures. Towards the end of that year, after throwing in that first teaching job, I had also finished a very brief career in advertising, returned to teaching as a casual, was working nights as a barman at the local and was writing my autobiographical novel, 'Don't Go to School With a Hangover and Lie on the Classroom Floor. Lie Standing up Instead'. As the mania built I changed the title to 'The Newest Testament' and my new job was to save the world. So in November I booked in to a special coaching clinic for the first time (if the metaphor is getting too extended ... a psychiatric clinic).

Remember that injury responds best to proper diagnosis and treatment. This first hospitalisation resulted in a misdiagnosis—paranoid schizophrenia—and treatment with Mellaril, an antipsychotic. But I didn't take it once I left hospital and six months later, walking the nights in my home city, I was diagnosed as manic depressive and prescribed lithium. I went back to full-time casual teaching at another school, stopped taking the lithium and lasted a year before they had to let me go.

Positional changes don't always prevent a recurrence of injury, however. Self-employment seemed a good option at this point. I signed up to sell herbal weight loss products, cosmetics and cleaning products. But I was the only one who got cleaned out. Then a publisher rejected my novel and my book of poems. So I hitchhiked from one job interview in the far north to another in the far south. Though I turned up late for that interview, I got the job, then turned up late for the job, lost the job and froze out in the open that night when I couldn't get a lift home or catch a horse. Soon it came to me again that my vocation really was to save the world. So I wasn't surprised to have a police escort from my then home to another psychiatric hospital. I figured with such an important job I needed protection.

A chronic injury sometimes requires a lifetime of treatment. I found the thought of ever going back to a psych institution intolerable, so I decided to take my lithium. I found my way back to teaching. The decision to keep taking my medication was one that allowed me to build a career in teaching that spanned two decades. I remained a full-time permanent teacher until, in the cloud of a severe depression, I decided to leave teaching. My doctor gave me three months' sick leave, so the cloud lifted and within two weeks I had returned to my recurrent job of saving the world. Up, up and away! I began emailing my solutions to the new Pope and it was only a matter of days before the ambulance came to take me to my newest 'coaching clinic'.

My observations from all this? Demonstrate your value as a utility player. One of the best things about being bipolar is the energy that you can bring to the workplace, as well as the creativity and ability to take on multiple challenges. During my teaching career I spent a long time as the union representative, I became involved in national educational research—authoring several research papers—I often worked as relieving head English teacher and I marked final year English for more than ten years. Keeping busy and in meaningful and fulfilling roles is important, as is being open to take on new challenges.

Believe in yourself and your ability. Negative talk is bad for your game. Bipolar is a word, not a sentence. The stigma you feel about your mood disorder can be the thing that holds you back the most in life and in the workplace. Learn to nurture your strengths and realise that everyone else out there has their own anxieties and uncertainties that they too must overcome. Increase the understanding of mood disorder among your coworkers by demonstrating how well you work. When you know the time is right, disclose your condition. Ideally, management should know too, but unfortunately a disclosure at this level may impact negatively on your career. This is a good time to talk to the coaching staff—your support team.

Your support team is important to maintaining your fitness. To remain well and to enjoy an uninterrupted career of almost twenty years as a high school teacher is something that I am proud of. Initially my support team was my immediate family—Mum, Dad, my brothers and sister. It also included those special people who had stayed close to me. Today it is all of these as well as my wife and two daughters. The best tackle of my career was to meet my wife in the workplace and then build a life together in the sun. Despite my family being witness to my disturbing behaviour during my manic episodes, I know we are closer for the experience. You need to be open, honest, loving and forgiving when your father or your husband becomes someone who frightens you. My medical team is vital too. A close, ongoing relationship with your GP is critical.

You have to keep getting up and moving forward to meet the opposition. After an episode, after the loss of another job, it is so hard to get up and out and going again, but it is essential. Sadly, I have had to creatively hide the gaps in my résumé in order to find work, but I am determined not to do that again.

Remember that there is life after 'football'. I now work as a disability support worker in a large residence not far from my home. My decision to finally leave teaching has been a good one. It has opened up so many new paths and possibilities. I take time most days to see the things of beauty around me, I subscribe to the therapies that are music and exercise, and I am publishing some poetry now. I have found time for myself, time for my family and time to find the work I really should be doing.

And I did recently get a job by including my mental health experience in my résumé. Not a job in the 'real' world—this will come—but working part-time in mental health respite. With my other work I have to watch that I don't take on too much—it is part of my nature, part of my illness, one of my weaknesses, one of my strengths.

Now approaching fifty, my defensive game remains strong and I still have a pretty good sidestep, but I know that I have to do a lot more training to keep fit and to continue to be selected for the field. **Stuart**

The individual and the organisation ultimately have the same goal: both 'sides' want to identify and develop the skills that coalesce into a productive alliance. Reflection, vocational tests, advisors and mentors can all sharpen up the individual's assessment of their capacities and the industries that are likely to be the best fit in terms of availability, stability and work pressure. And organisations will attract employees who better match their needs when jobs are clearly defined and described.

11
Work is a contact sport
Contracts that encourage fair play

❝ I believe the three major areas we need to look at within the workplace are staff training and education, management training and education, and organisational culture.
Alex

An employee offers some suggestions for how the workplace could be improved. His suggestions range from the simple through to more complex and costly changes.

❝ Here are some workplace factors which are able to be addressed and can go a long way to building morale for all in the workplace. The following overlap and interact, but improvements can include:

- architectural features—such as bright lights in winter; healthy air, especially preventing 'sick building syndrome' and pollution; plants; paintings; awareness of ambient noise levels; and provision for some privacy
- physical spaces—large organisations could benefit from providing, say, a gymnasium, swimming pool, board games room, library, and garden with lawns and seating
- better human relations—for example, honesty and transparency of communications especially during economic turmoil, and the encouragement for all directors, management and employees to ideally look out for and care about each other and themselves (as Tolstoy said, 'Each of us is responsible for everything and to everyone')
- attention to industrial issues—for example, job security, working hours, salaries, retrenchment, redundancy and retirement

- awareness of psychological issues—such as job satisfaction and sense of purpose, autonomy and control, confidentiality, policies on private telephone/email/internet usage, and an egalitarian dining room and social club
- helpful OH&S policies—including those that cover alcohol and drugs, cigarette smoking, caffeinism, meal breaks, excessive working hours and shift work, and in larger organisations, an officer trained in psychiatric/psychological issues
- miscellaneous issues—such as programs for improved health that encourage exercise, stress resistance and relief, health checks and vaccinations
- with severe mood episodes, sick leave may be needed; in less severe episodes, reduced working hours and/or lessened responsibilities may be appropriate—sensitive liaison with treating professionals is highly desirable but only with the person's consent. **Jake**

Changes to the workplace that create a more friendly, supportive and flexible environment don't have to be costly or difficult. Some organisations offered the following suggestions to make the workplace more 'family-friendly':

- schedule meetings within normal working hours
- ensure that staff take their annual leave in the year that it is due
- allow staff to take annual leave in single days
- allow leave without pay for cultural purposes
- develop policies regarding unpaid leave for employees who care for children with disabilities, elderly relatives or people with other special needs

- negotiate flexible start and finish times
- establish quality part-time work or job-sharing opportunities
- discourage (except in exceptional circumstances) weekend work and staying back late in the office
- allow staff to have a say in rostering arrangements, for example, base them on school terms
- introduce 'make-up time' so staff can make up hours if they need to attend an appointment
- allow staff to use their sick leave entitlements to care for family members
- broaden the definition of 'family' to include more distant relatives for the purposes of bereavement leave
- provide information on local contacts to help staff find child care, school holiday care and elder/respite care
- provide an emergency phone for employees to contact family members (for instance, if they are worried about an older child sick at home)
- allow staff to use work mobile phones for emergency family reasons
- introduce a 'keep in touch' plan for staff on maternity leave
- hold a 'bring your child to work' day, or a family picnic day
- introduce a workplace policy for employees who are breastfeeding
- provide facilities such as family rooms for employees with young children
- extend social events such as happy hours to families and partners

- put work and family issues on the agenda to discuss at the next round of negotiations for your workplace agreement
- consider the needs of partners and families in any relocations and movements
- include a summary of your company's work and family policy in a letter of offer to new employees
- establish a workplace mentoring program
- ensure that your workplace has clear contractual obligations that perform the dual task of communicating to the worker the expectations of the business and, if there is a breach, enabling the enforcement of the expectation.[1]

MENTAL HEALTH AT WORK

Those who study populations at work agree that preventative health measures to reduce stress and to identify incipient mental health problems are ultimately beneficial. A document from Canada, *Mental Health at Work*[2], covers some preventative strategies. **Primary prevention** is understood as identifying and dealing with the root causes of stress within the workplace; **secondary prevention** concentrates more on the personal characteristics and work habits of individuals; and **tertiary prevention** emerges when the individual is experiencing job-related mental illness and involves mechanisms for best managing an individual who has developed such problems.

Some of the more detailed suggestions from *Mental Health at Work* include the following:

Primary prevention strategies

Regular team or group meetings to:

- clarify roles, responsibilities and powers
- specify expectations, goals and objectives
- give recognition, social support and feedback
- disseminate information about activities in the organisation
- discuss workplace problems and solutions
- open up dialogue with supervisors and colleagues
- assess fairness of workload.

Encourage participative management to:

- improve relationships between supervisors and employees
- increase employees' participation in decisions
- enhance employees' loyalty.

Offer training to develop knowledge and skills to help:

- advance careers and recognise achievement
- prepare for more responsibilities
- enhance a sense of mastery and autonomy.

Analyse positions and tasks to:

- assess and distribute workloads
- clarify roles, responsibilities and powers related to each position
- specify expectations, goals and objectives
- reduce work-related risks.

In addition, conduct an annual evaluation of employees' contributions.

Secondary prevention strategies

Include articles on mental health at work in the in-house newspaper, and host information and awareness activities such as:

- conferences on the physical and behavioural symptoms of work-related mental health problems
- 'lunch and learn' sessions on the causes of mental health problems at work
- seminars on the prevention of work-related mental health problems
- workshops on managing and adapting to change.

Run skills development programs about:

- stress and time management
- conflict and problem management and resolution
- balancing personal and professional obligations
- meditation, yoga or other relaxation techniques
- healthy eating
- physical exercise
- smoking cessation and aspects of drug and alcohol use.

Tertiary prevention strategies

These could include a return-to-work program, 'peer help' networks, and an employee assistance program that can assess mental health needs and broker referrals to specialised resources. It is important to build in sufficient follow-up and support.

At the broader level, companies that are feted are those whose ethics and standards are genuinely central to the organisation's view of itself. Business magazines frequently list the best organisations to work for and it is no coincidence that these organisations are also characterised by originality, high productivity and low staff turnover. Examples include NetApp, Boston Consulting Group, Google, Cisco Systems, Goldman Sachs, Adobe Systems and various not-for-profits, to pick just a few from the 'Top 100'. The US company Enron provides an interesting case study of the effect of prevailing culture, when over a few years it morphed from excellent corporate 'citizen' into rogue company. Starting from top management down, the feedback loop of what was expected and sanctioned in an aggressive pursuit of profit made many complicit in its slide into corruption.

In respected organisations, values are clearly stated and overtly practised (and good values are found to be good for business). The boss is visible and knows the employees, and the employees understand the company's goals and that it is built to last. The workforce is trusted and autonomous within the bounds of what is being produced. Suggestions and criticisms are encouraged and acted upon. The work environment also includes benefits and flexibility appropriate to the particular workforce. Such a backdrop supports and encourages workers and enables them to present with any incapacity at an early stage, when it can most effectively be managed.

While mood disorders in the workplace are more prevalent, whether that be due to better diagnosis and/or more stressful workplace conditions, there is also better targeted support and treatment to help those affected to regain their previous good health. The earlier such treatment is sought, the more effective it is. Giving 'permission'—via workplace education and destigmatisation programs and a general climate of trust—for a worker or manager (or boss) to recognise that they need help and to be able to ask for it promotes better productivity, not a culture of entitlement. It is essential, however, that any disclosure of disability at work be handled sensitively and confidentially, preferably by the individual's line manager or boss.

Organisational support to promote a tolerant and resilient workplace has been found to bring solid returns: increased productivity, reduced absenteeism and lower staff turnover, but such a culture will not take root unless it is genuinely supported at all levels in the organisation, particularly at the top.

12
Stories from the change room
People tell about managing their
mood disorder

The accounts that follow are from people who have tackled their mood disorder and successfully continued in, or re-entered, the workforce. In order to do this they have taken a number of steps. First, they (or relatives, friends or fellow workers) have recognised that they are 'off their game'. Next, they have decided that it is possible to do something about this—often despite the way they feel—as depression can whisper, 'This is just the way life is and always will be and neither you nor I can do anything about it,' and mania shouts, 'Wow! I feel better than fabulous and what are all these kill-joys nagging me about? It's their problem, not mine.' The following people accepted that there was a problem, had faith that it could be ameliorated and took responsibility for seeking help. They have each put together a unique self-management plan after assessing information and advice and pursuing treatment for their condition. They have been stalwart about persisting—with the help of others—in seeking and adopting strategies for managing their condition.

MY SHINY OFFICE JOB AND ME

My shiny office job is travel editing. I shift sentences around like pins on a map. There is a vicarious thrill to all these far-off places. Sudan, Bangkok, Virginia, Laos. Someone with poorer grammar than mine has been to these places and is counting on me to make them as shiningly evocative as possible.

So I do. And now here I am, sitting in my office, wanting to have fixed things, knowing that I haven't. I think about the odds, the statistics and what they say. How many other people in my converted warehouse want to take a running jump off the top of the building? How many cry in the toilets, in secret? How many, like me, can't always seem to find the emotional energy for tears? How many have stones in their pockets and can feel the water rising? Five per cent? Ten? Twenty?

I try to pick them. It becomes a game, a morbid one—who here in this office is clinically depressed? Winner gets to go home an hour early and cry in bed. I invent other games, too, more helpful ones—my mother would say 'coping mechanisms' and she'd be right. I set myself tiny deadlines and try to beat them. I predict what colour the girl next to me will wear every day, and invent outlandish, non-office-appropriate costumes for her.

I steal a teaspoon of sugar and a teabag every night, keeping them in little packets in my handbag. I transfer them to glass jars in my kitchen. Each day is a soupy morass, blending into the one before it, but gradually the levels of tea and sugar began to rise. I discover that others, furtively, are engaging in subversive activities too. One writer has invented a fake country and adds details to it every time he gets frustrated with the real ones. This makes me feel oddly gleeful.

Of course, I work as well. Rearranging words, smoothing them into a better order, is the best part of my day. I think it keeps me sane. Maybe it *makes* me sane. **Tania**

TACKLING MOOD DISORDERS IN THE WORKPLACE; OR, MANAGING YOUR WORK COLLEAGUES' OUTDATED OPINIONS ABOUT MENTAL HEALTH
Surviving the office (particularly when you're a bit like me and not quite so interested in normal social cues about what you do and don't say to your boss) is a bit like

filming a series of *Survivor* on the Pakistani border with ten Western tourists as the unwitting participants. It's only a matter of time before someone steps on an unexploded mine. Throw in an (as yet) undiagnosed mood disorder and you've got a recipe for paranoia, underperformance, histrionics and, inevitably, disaster.

Nine to five, Monday to Friday, was only really a small part of managing my bipolar disorder. I was also trying not to get dumped, be deleted from my friends' lives entirely and manage a best friend who was majoring in women's studies and social work and not backward in coming forward regarding her opinions of psychiatry. (Seriously, if I was going to have to endure her opining for a great deal longer, I'd just kill myself and be done with it!)

That being said, work time was hardly insignificant. One would argue that it had actually become entirely critical, given that I had used all my sick days and had just started missing chunks of the working week—too depressed to turn up and too embarrassed to call in sick.

It was fortuitous then that my current boss was one of those sensitive New Age guy types (either that or working in an office full of women, the oestrogen had finally gotten to him). Anyway, he had started to twig that something wasn't right and had promptly called on the services of an outside contractor who specialised in rehabilitating those public servants who had taken leave of their remaining marbles (it was the public service after all, I was lucky a steering committee hadn't been established).

The long and the short of it was that, after a quick visit to my GP, who had decided that I was indeed a Woman on the Edge, I was prescribed a holiday 'starting *now*' and a referral to a psychiatrist.

In the new year, on return to the workplace, I found that the suicidal thoughts, nausea and dizziness were nothing in comparison to the stifling feeling of having so many people managing my mental health—as though I were a patient at the Buttery. Worse still, I wasn't 100 per cent sold on the fact that I was the craziest person in the equation.

There was my psychiatrist, who had clearly spent far too much time at university listening to the sound of his own voice; two departmental social workers who *hadn't* spent enough time at university (or wherever Those People went these days); my rehabilitation case worker (a clinical psychologist who was actually the same age as me, thereby killing any assumption I may have made regarding her superior wisdom); my GP (a bloke who was so laid-back he was almost horizontal, except for the fact that he couldn't seem to understand how he had come to be so unlucky as to have me darkening his doorstep for the last eighteen months); and my private psychologist who had, in an odd coincidence, started seeing an ex-lover of mine—a shy young girl who, if not for the compulsive carving up of her left arm and the borderline personality disorder, would have made quite a nice girlfriend for him.

Outside of this case management team there were also a few others in this office jungle who warranted closer inspection . . .

These ranged from the security guard—who was so tightly wound up about the fact that my security pass (and its gravely unflattering photo) was hidden in my bag rather than emblazoned around my neck by virtue of a self-important lanyard that he wouldn't have noticed if Osama Bin Laden had scanned in with the division manager's severed hand in a plastic bag—right up to the division manager himself, whose idea of management was to enter the corral of some unsuspecting chump, give a verbal spray and disappear as quickly as he had arrived. My workplace itself was perilously close to The Edge. It made me think of that Gary Larsen comic with the large brick building entitled 'Crisis Clinic' simultaneously on fire and heading over a waterfall.

The point I'm making is, you might have six mental health care professionals managing you and a piece of paper that certifies you, but chances are you are probably the least insane person in the building. Furthermore, once you start talking about your experience, they will all come crawling out of the woodwork. And when that starts happening, here are a few pointers to keep in mind:

- Surviving the office jungle was best described to me by an older friend who'd spend a number of years as senior advisor to the then-Minister for Indigenous Affairs. You need to know 'who's who in the zoo'. Roughly translated in this situation: get support— whether it be formally through a case worker, or informally through colleagues or a boss whom you see as an ally. Don't isolate yourself: paranoia will set in, and quite frankly that always ends in tears.
- While on the topic of tears, a well-placed tear is fine, people's humanity means that even the toughest nut will soften. But seriously—a well-placed tear. Leave the racking sobs and the keening wails of worthlessness for friends, families and even the bottom of a vodka bottle (although I wouldn't recommend the vodka route).

- If you have the luxury of any sick days left, and aren't going to get sacked because you take them, take the time off when you need to. It's all well and good knowing you've got bats in the belfry but coming to terms with this knowledge is where the real skill comes in. *Do not* come to work when you are having a bad day. It just takes the resources away from the work at hand because everybody's managing *you* and the fact that you look like you're about to tie the fax machine to your leg and jump out the window. Go home. You snivelling at your desk isn't helping anyone.

- Have some compassion for those who are trying to say and do the right thing but may be making a pig's ear of it in the process. I have met very few people in my life who are intentionally trying to cause others pain. The problem is, I think, for every one in four people who suffer a mental illness at some point in their lives, the other three have likely got no bloody idea what it means. Unless you're cutting your wrists at your desk, claiming to talk in tongues, or walking in with your knickers on your head, chances are your mood disorder means you are quite intelligent, relatively charming and too paranoid to leave the house looking anything less than sharp enough to cut glass. And sadly, most people's idea of poor mental health involves that Helfgott chap playing the piano in a maniacal fashion and jumping around on a trampoline with no underwear on. If this isn't you, you are probably going to face an uphill battle getting people to understand how hard it really is. But persist.

- And finally, a piece of advice that is applicable
  not only to the workplace but always relevant as
  you start to 'come out' about your mood disorder.
  Everyone (and I mean *everyone*) is going to have a
  theory on what will work. Whether it's meditation,
  exercise, alkalising for health, liver cleansing, fresh
  juicing, St John's Wort, Rescue Remedy, chamomile,
  deep breathing, repeating empowering mantras and
  just generally lighting some incense, but ... *know
  thyself*. **Janey**

OUTRUNNING THE BLACK DOG

On the way to work that morning I kept the windows
wound up. I could see the mist from the black dog's sickly
breath form on my windscreen as I drove faster, trying to
outrun him. I should have known it was useless. Reaching
into the glove box, I popped the pills I had forgotten to
take at breakfast and cranked up the happy tunes on the
stereo. Yet still he chased me. And what was worse was
that he was gaining. I guessed it was a matter of hours at
best before I felt his weight on my chest, forcing out my
breath and demanding I yield. I could feel it, see it, smell
it, but there was nothing I could do. So I did what any
mature adult would do in such a situation. I ignored it and
hoped it would go away.

My black dog feeds on any disturbances in routine. I
like to think I call the shots but, like soggy-trousered Canute,
that is mere vanity. He circles tirelessly in the darkness,
often just outside the twinkling campfires of reason. I hear
him bay for blood, but have procedures in place to stop
him getting too close. Well, that's generally the pattern.
Sometimes his strength will catch me off guard and I am

down, forced to play 'fetch' with the gnawed ball that is my self-worth. At these times I just hope he has his fun and goes away. My wife is the ultimate rodeo clown, running in circles and shouting distraction in the hope she can break his concentration long enough for me to escape over the railing. Unfortunately, sometimes the funny hats and coloured pantaloons don't cut it and I am left alone in the ring to suffer at his whim.

I expect others to be able to see the dog and his effect on me, but that's not always fair, nor possible. I tell my friends and family about him, but they don't really understand that not all animals are the same. They talk about the dog they had as a kid, or one their flatmate had that used to mope around the house shitting on the carpet. 'It's not the same!' I cry internally, but I know that some things just have to be experienced. So I pick myself up again and put Band-aids on the bites and look forward to a better day. **Carl**

PROPHECY

I never thought I would hear such a thing from a psychiatrist. I had already been off work for some weeks, my mind and body having shut down. At first I thought I was just exhausted or burned out but then thoughts of suicide morphed into detailed plans. I remember little else about that first consultation apart from the psychiatrist's unusual prediction. I was 42 years old and had worked in the health system for twenty years. I felt that I had given my all, and that work and I would never be reunited. To hear him tell me that I would be 'a better social worker' after this experience was an affront. I remember thinking that he was completely off the mark. I was convinced I would never work again, and even if I did, social work would be the last thing I would do. My right leg twitched for want of kicking his shins at even mentioning such a preposterous idea.

I lived and worked in a semi-rural area and in my community social work role I had contact with health professionals across the region. We often spoke about the disadvantage of working for the same health service that one day we might require to access as a patient, but I visualised a broken limb, not a broken mind. Fifteen years ago the stigma about mental illness had only started to be addressed. Even with my professional knowledge of depressive illness I still felt embarrassed and guilty for having been weak and allowing myself to become ill. 'If I can't help myself then how can I help others?' was a constant self-talk put-down. Finding a psychiatrist with whom I had no previous contact or clients in common was challenging. It was a further devastating blow to be told that I required admission to the clinic where I frequently referred clients, and where I knew many of the staff. On the day of my admission I found myself running out in terror at the prospect of being admitted by a nurse I knew well. This action of a depressed mind even further embarrassed the underlying healthy mind, a tussle that took some years to overcome.

With time, medication and support I was eventually able to prove my psychiatrist right. In combination these were the three elements that he and others provided. I now believe them to be the cornerstones to recovering from any depressive illness.

Time alone can be a healer, or so my psychiatrist told me, referring to a past century of spending months in a bath-chair on the Mediterranean. However, I had a family to care for, a mortgage to pay and, though I couldn't contemplate it at the time, a job to keep. The time I needed was time away from work and responsibilities, time to recover without pressures, in my own time. I was fortunate that an accumulation of unused sick leave saw me through the three months that I needed before I was well enough to resume work.

Imipramine was the medication of choice back then. Very soon it began to take effect, stopping the self-destructive thoughts. As the dose increased to a therapeutic level it allowed me to re-engage with those around me and to hold social conversations. Gradually my functioning began to resemble my former self, and apart from the side-effect of a constantly dry mouth, the medication suited me well. I maintained that dose for many months following my return to work and mental health.

The third ingredient of my recovery was the support that I received from the psychiatrist, my close associates and, in terms of returning to work, my workplace. Ongoing appointments with a psychiatrist who was prepared to talk as well as prescribe were vitally important. As so often occurs, those who are listeners, either by trade or nature (often both), find themselves rarely heard. I had developed great expertise in deflecting conversations about myself back onto the inquirer, so my psychiatric consultations gave a new opportunity to focus on myself. Family, friends and colleagues who accepted, understood and gave me the time I needed to recover were highly valued. Judgement, intolerance and impatience from others were all experiences that tended to push me back down. This often came from surprising sources, resulting in some friendships and associations being severed.

As for work, a planned gradual return was implemented that not only addressed my hours of work but also my duties. Bit by bit as my confidence was regained I took back more responsibilities until I returned to full capacity. Had I been required to return to full duties immediately I firmly believe that I would not still be working fifteen years on.

In order to be a better social worker I do not advocate that I (or any other therapists) need to experience the client's issues. There is no place in my work manual for 'I know how you feel'. However, I do believe that having experienced and recovered from a major depressive illness, my understanding of the nuances of the illness and its management are heightened. In this way my psychiatrist was correct. I do consider myself to be a better social worker on three levels: in myself as a worker, in my work with clients, and in my role as a manager.

Most importantly, my experience has enabled me to monitor my own mental health more effectively. Instead of struggling, denying, masking and trying to keep going against all odds, I now understand my moods and thought processes. This enables me to take action at an early stage to prevent falling down the slippery slope towards illness. For fifteen years I have been able to avoid a recurrence of depression. But nothing is ever as straightforward as we may wish. Just when I thought it would never happen again I found myself back with disordered thoughts and suicide plans, despite my attention to self-care actions. This time I swiftly sought medical assistance, so instead of three months off work it was only three weeks before the medication gave me the assistance I needed to begin functioning again. This time I am monitored by my GP whose treatment of depression is assisted by access to Black Dog Institute resources online. I have learnt another important lesson from this: that is, despite my best endeavours to protect my mental health, there is always the chance that body chemistry will fail. Early recognition of a mood disorder is the key to reducing the impact of illness.

In my work I now have a better understanding of depression and I can identify details that were previously hidden to me. I can work more effectively with people who are denying their symptoms and I can encourage more appropriately their step-by-step improvements. I can understand the turbulent nature of their journey and its impact on the whole of their life, including the impact of negative attitudes towards people with a mental illness. My journey will always be unique, as will everyone else's. Those who helped me the most were able to acknowledge and understand this. In turn I pay great attention to my clients' unique experiences and circumstances while at the same time highlighting the commonly shared elements in a way meaningful to them. I can also acknowledge that there can be positive outcomes associated with depression. It enables anyone who has travelled the journey to recognise the signposts, should we go that way again. In this way we can build our own map, the better to avoid relapse and manage future episodes of depression.

The third way my own experience has been useful relates to my role as a manager. What helped me to return to being an effective worker was the flexibility of work hours and duties and the understanding and support from my manager. I was able to work within my capacity, only extending this when I felt able to maintain it. This is a practice that I now support as a manager myself. When a mental illness is identified I discuss what will work best for the person, trying to understand their unique needs. This, of course, requires trust on both sides and an attitude that excludes judgement. With this trust comes the capacity to develop strategies that suit the worker's capacity. These should be regularly reviewed to remain relevant. At the same time it is equally important to avoid appearing overly concerned, as this can undermine the worker's confidence. Although it can have an impact on work output, my experience is that a short-term reduction is easier to manage than a permanent withdrawal of a worker's service.

I can't say whether it is despite my psychiatrist's affronting prophecy or because of it, but I now agree that my experience of depression has added to my life, not only as a social worker. Whichever way you look at it, there is indeed 'life in the old (black) dog yet'! **Sandra**

CHASING WHITE RABBITS—BIPOLARS, BEWARE OF NEWTON'S OTHER LAW

Now we reach an aspect of bipolar disorder that is intensely mortifying—the chasing of white rabbits. It is usually a necessity for people with bipolar disorder to conceal their thoughts and feelings from others. The capacity to think in ways that lack logic and have no basis in reality is something I loathe so much I have never spoken of it. I call it 'wrong-thinking' because it is not delusional but rather 'off-kilter'. I have never thought that

I am a supermodel, or spent money because I believe I am a millionaire. Instead, at the peak of either depression or mania I tend to perceive things that are not there. I am easily hurt in social settings because I misread other people's communications. As I move from the upper/lower end of the mood spectrum I realise I was wrong.

This is a dangerous phase socially. I become the Queen of Hearts: 'Off with your head!' I have destroyed relationships in this mode that never needed to die. Newton has a law: 'To every action there is an equal and opposite reaction.' People with bipolar disorder must avoid this principle in social and work settings at all costs. In a phase of wrong-thinking this law will harm you and your reputation. If an issue arises at work about which I feel negative I have learnt to disengage. Delay communication and decision-making to a later date. If my feelings remain strong then, in all likelihood, they are real. If my feelings have changed, then I have averted a scene that just didn't need to happen. Relationships remain intact and so does my self-respect. **Talia**

ONE DAY IN NOVEMBER

I remember that day in November 2006 as if it were yesterday.

I somehow got myself ready and got to work. I turned on my computer and an error message flashed up on the screen, 'NOT RESPONDING'. I wondered if it was some kind of sign. My phone rang and I reacted as if it were a gunshot. My heart was racing and I was trembling. I let it ring out and asked the receptionist to take messages for me for the rest of the day. I sat there and stared right through my computer. I felt like crying, but I had no idea why.

A colleague commented that I had lost weight and I looked unwell; others nodded in concurrence. I tottered back to my desk to Google my symptoms: lack of concentration, agitated, sensitive to sound, unable to multitask, poor memory, disrupted sleep, nausea, constant fatigue, headaches and jaw pain. I'd eliminated the amygdala tumour, but was it the early signs of some kind of psychotic disorder? I'd studied psychology, I knew about these things. I made an appointment with my GP—the third that month. This time I was going to be firm and tell him I wanted to know what was wrong with me. This had been going on for six months, and while all the tests so far had come back negative, I thought he must have been missing something.

At that point I was exhausted from pretending, I couldn't fake the smiles anymore. My voice was monotone to the point where I couldn't stand the sound of it myself. The only answer I had when people asked me 'What's the matter?' was 'I don't know.' I did not know what was wrong with me, but I knew it was something serious. I started to think about what I wanted to do with all my belongings when I died. I wanted to make sure everything was in order so my family were not burdened by it.

My sister explained my symptoms to the doctor, while I just concentrated on breathing. 'I am writing you a medical certificate to have some time off work. You are going through a major depressive episode.' No! It must be a mistake. This is not what depression is like—and what do I have to be depressed about anyway?

The following week was a blur. I felt like I was trapped in a bubble, with only just enough air to keep me alive. I was completely disconnected from the rest of the world. I was angry that people could carry on with their lives as if nothing was wrong. My sister almost had to hold me down and force the medication down my throat. The side-effects were ghastly: pounding headaches, a dry mouth and nightmares worse than any horror movie. For weeks I suffered bizarre sensations of detachment and depersonalisation. It's a place I never want to return to.

But here I am, more than two years later, working full-time in a job I love and feeling positive about the future. How did I get here? Well, I am going to share that with you, in the hope that I can help someone else recover from depression and maintain their employment.

Support

Fortunately for me I work in a field where I have a lot of contacts and a lot of support, and I live in a city where I can access good practitioners. I also have a very supportive family and an understanding partner. I don't know how people get through without them. I must say though, there were a few unwelcome comments early on, such as 'Pick yourself up' and 'Snap out of it'. Anyone with depression will understand how frustrating this is. I also had a great GP who referred me to a psychiatrist and a psychologist, and who reviewed me on a regular basis until I stabilised. He managed my return to work, giving me time to recover but also encouraging me to return as soon as I was able, as being able to contribute to a team and achieve small goals at work gave me a purpose.

Treatment

Medication got me to a point where I could function and explore other forms of treatment. I have been taking anti-depressants for two years now. Despite the first few weeks of side-effects and adjusting the dose a few times along the way, I have had no other issues with medication, and I encourage people to be patient while they adjust to it if they need medication.

I did cognitive behavioural therapy (CBT) with a therapist and also read many books based on this technique and completed the Australian National University's Mood Gym, which is an innovative online program. I found books written by Louise Hay to be extremely uplifting, and a book called *Change Your Thinking* by Sarah Edelman (ABC Books, 2006) was informative and practical. I was given a CBT worksheet to assist me to challenge my thoughts, and to begin with I did this on a daily basis. This also helped me to gain an insight into why I am susceptible to depression.

I believe things turned around for me when I realised I had to relearn two of the most basic of life skills; how to breathe and how to think. I had a distorted way of thinking, and had developed a pattern of breathing which was very shallow, rapid and at times erratic. The breath is the best tool we have to influence our body and mind. Learning to meditate and how to do yoga really made a difference to my breathing, and my overall health and wellbeing.

Exercise and diet

Exercise and diet were crucial to my recovery. I forced myself to swim every day and this took a huge effort. During the early stages I could only manage one or two laps, and getting myself to the pool and home again was a full day's work for me. I aimed to eat every two hours with lots of fresh fruits and vegetables, and also took Omega 3 supplements, which are believed to assist people suffering depression. All this was difficult as food did not taste pleasant and I did not have an appetite. This routine was important when I returned to work, and I even resorted to setting a reminder on my email calendar to remind me to eat!

Managing at work

I also set myself reminders to change tasks every half hour, to assist with my concentration. Gradually this increased to every hour once I began feeling better. I alternated using the mouse with my right and left hand as this is believed to assist with activating the two brain hemispheres. It has been established that the right brain, which is connected with a person's intuitive, creative and holistic faculties, is linked to left-hand movements, while the left brain, whose functions are logical, analytical and rational, is linked to the right hand. I walked for 30 minutes in my lunch break, even if it was at a snail's pace, and I parked my car in a place where I was forced to go out and move it every three hours.

My 'work management plan'

All of the above were set out on a document called a 'work management plan'. At the top of the plan I set out goals: short, medium and long term. The goals were very basic to begin with, things like practising yoga and meditation daily, or increasing my hours at work. It was important to develop goals to enable me to see progress and to have something to motivate me and work towards.

I developed the work management plan with a case manager from the health and safety department of the company I was working for, and also an external rehabilitation provider, appointed and paid for by the employer. I worked for a large federal government agency; however,

I understand in private industry and in smaller depart-
ments they may not be as readily available. Nonetheless,
all employers have a duty of care to their employees, and
you might be pleasantly surprised at the support offered
when you are honest and open with your employer about
your condition.

I commenced back at work on half days to enable
me to attend appointments, to exercise and to rest. I
then gradually increased my hours and worked full days
on Monday, Wednesday and Friday and half days on
Tuesday and Thursday. This ensured that I was able to
work effectively for the time I was at work, and also had
the time to work on improving my health.

One of my long-term goals was to do volunteer work
in the field of mental health when I recovered, and I have
been doing this for about six months now. This involves
speaking to high school students about my experience and
giving them information on where to go for help if they find
themselves in the same position. I find this very rewarding,
and if it helps one person then it is a success. I concentrate
on having a work/life balance, and I have an employer
who supports this.

I still have nightmares and I still grind my teeth, much
to my partner's disgust! I often have to challenge my
thoughts, and I have been told I will take medication for
the rest of my life. But I believe we all have challenges to
face in life, and this is my path. I have learnt a lot about
myself and about life. I am healthy and happy, and now
I wouldn't change a thing. **Prakesh**

❛ WALKING THE LINE
As a nurse with a bipolar illness, I sometimes cross that
metaphorical boundary line that separates nurses from

patients. Despite education on psychiatric disorders and experience with caring for patients with mental health problems, many nurses respond negatively to colleagues who have a mood disorder. Nursing is a profession that commonly requires team work to provide good patient care. Consequently, if you have depression or a bipolar illness you will need to develop practices to ensure role expectations are achieved and that good working relationships are developed and sustained.

To tell or not to tell, that is the question

The level of awareness that other employees have of your illness is often a major influence on the techniques that you choose to ensure a satisfactory work performance. Consequently, most of the following discussion surrounds the issue of disclosure. If coworkers are unaware of your situation, you have the option of disclosing your mental health problems or deliberately withholding that information. Some workers believe that a person is obliged to reveal their illness at the workplace. However, I think that disclosure is not a necessity, it is a strategy which may minimise work stress. Nevertheless, deciding whether to disclose is not an easy one, because there is no guaranteed positive outcome. Put simply, when you're considering how a person will react to your disclosure and the subsequent impact on your work experiences, there are many 'what ifs' in the equation.

If you decide to disclose, it is wise to consider the timing. Possibilities include when commencing new employment, returning to work following an absence due to depression or hypomania, and when developing or experiencing symptoms of an acute episode of the illness. An opportune time might be when mental health issues are a topic of conversation. When you start a new job, there are benefits if you delay disclosure. For instance, additional time to establish your position as a 'team player' is likely to minimise the potential for a judgemental reaction to your disclosed 'secret', and coworkers are more likely to respond positively if they recognise changes in your behaviour or thinking.

How much is too much?

It is also essential to think about who needs to be advised of your health problem and how much knowledge is required. If you're uncertain about who should be informed or if you feel uncomfortable telling people, you could try selective disclosure. That is, test the waters with someone whom you think you can trust not to inform others and who will be supportive. If you do receive a positive response, that person may assist you to tell others.

There are situations when you don't have a choice for a planned decision to disclose. For instance, coworkers may be unaware of your situation but recognise changes in your conduct and respond with hostility. Conversely, they may seek an explanation for your behaviour and offer support. There is no prescription for how you manage these situations. In each circumstance it would be reasonable (and hopeful) to think that disclosure would be the appropriate strategy to use. In my experience, most people, whether or not they have a mood disorder, find the opportunity to talk about sensitive or embarrassing issues and to get them out in the open is often preferable to the stress of holding them in. Disclosure is a journey into unknown territory but I've found that if people know the reason for your behaviour, more often than not it will lead to acceptance and peer support. However, given the widespread stigma around mental illness, support can't be guaranteed!

Write it down

When you are developing or experiencing symptoms of a mood disorder, or even when you are mentally healthy, anxiety and panic can occur when you feel pressured about your performance. A written plan and self-monitoring (assessing your progress against the plan) can assist with organising and prioritising your work-load. However, there are difficulties with this technique. Constantly checking and the effort required to stick to the timetable are often stressful and time-consuming and therefore counteract the intentions of the work plan. In addition, colleagues may resent that you work at a slower pace than everyone else, particularly if they are required to assist you.

A 'return to work plan'

If you have an extended absence from work for mental health reasons, I recommend negotiating a 'return to work plan' with your employer or manager. The aim of the agreement is to minimise your stress and maximise your self-confidence. The plan could include reduced and specific work hours, a period of decreased responsibility, and a 'buddy' for support.

An action plan will assist with minimising disruptions to your work life. A documented management plan may be useful for future episodes. Developing the instructions need not be a solo endeavour; other people such as your therapist, carer or a family member can contribute. The key people or service providers identified in the plan need to be aware of their role and agree to be involved. If your manager or your employer is willing to participate, it may be beneficial to include them in the plan. For example, if you are absent from work, a manager's responsibility could be confirming leave entitlements, ensuring that you receive any payments due and making certain that relevant paperwork is completed.

Meetings, meetings, meetings!

If your work involves attending meetings or working closely with others, it is always helpful to document issues that you want to discuss, as memory is often affected by a mental illness. Likewise, writing notes during a meeting or shortly afterwards can assist your recollection of the discussion, especially if you are required to act on issues that were raised. If you are unable to record the meeting or you feel self-conscious using these strategies, making light of having a 'terrible memory' or 'getting old' may help the situation. Simply stating that 'I'm having a bad day today' is also a good tactic if you feel comfortable with people with whom you work. Another successful technique that I have used is asking the people I'm working with to write down what is discussed—and making light of it by saying that I can't listen, think and write at the same time.

Medication

Side-effects of psychotropic medication such as nausea, tremor and weight gain can be troublesome. If you have control over aspects of your employment, changing your dress and hair styles can disguise your weight. This strategy may also increase your self-esteem and reduce the risk of being stigmatised (because of your size) by your colleagues.

Night-time medication can make it difficult to get out of bed in the morning, and cause sluggishness. Morning tiredness can be overcome if your employer is willing to adjust the time that you start work. If you don't have this option, working an afternoon shift can help with the issue of morning lethargy. A different strategy is to discuss your medication concerns with your doctor. It may be possible to adjust your medication regimen. For example, alter the time that you take medication and modify the dosage to accommodate your employment commitments. Sometimes this is a preferred approach, as it doesn't attract unwanted attention of the sort that would occur if you changed your work hours.

Workplace relationships

Most people view social relationships as a necessary part of life. If your workplace is one where employees take impromptu cigarette or coffee breaks, even if you do not smoke you can use this 'time out' as a stress-reducing tool and an opportunity to engage with others. Relating to colleagues during meal breaks is a technique I use to increase my self-esteem and self-confidence. Some workplaces have regular social occasions outside of work hours. If you are able to attend these events, it will assist you to feel part of the team and at the same time will reinforce your position as a team member.

Knowledge is empowering

A fundamental strategy if you have a mood disorder is learning to recognise triggers and signs of an approaching depressive or manic episode. I choose to work part-time hours because full-time employment has a harmful influence on my mood. For similar reasons, I don't do night duty as it has a negative effect on my body clock and subsequently triggers depression or hypomania.

Clearly, there are no 'one size fits all' strategies to tackle mood disorders at the workplace. Nevertheless, there are many more techniques than those presented here. You can access other suggestions from many sources, especially participation in support groups, reading self-help books and learning from personal accounts of survival at work. Reputable internet sites such as SANE, beyondblue and the Black Dog Institute, in Australia, also provide information on coping with mood disorders.

Good luck with walking the line! **Jodie**

We close by suggesting again that, in managing the impact of depression or bipolar disorder in the workplace, there is no single strategy for implementation or closure. The severity of the individual's mood disorder, the extent to which they can discuss it openly, and the degree to which they feel obliged to mask or deny its existence all have the capacity to impact at work. Similarly, the workplace 'culture' (both intrinsically and when 'tested' by an employee whose health is impaired) can vary considerably—from monitoring and supporting people through to intolerance of any employee judged as compromising work or output.

In addition to such general or systemic issues, each situation is unique. The employee may choose to be open and disclose their condition, or deny or rationalise any limitations; the employer may prioritise the wellbeing of workers, or focus narrowly on output, with the end justifying the means, and display a harsh attitude to any worker with limitations.

Ideally, the individual with a mood disorder will be committed to performing as well as they are able, find work helpful (both in itself and as a distraction that does lift their mood to some degree), have an employer who is sensitive to their needs, and flexible when required, and be part of an organisation that demonstrates 'core values' rather than merely claiming such values.

While there is no single strategy to promote effective functioning, by detailing some of the nuances and complexities—and providing the wisdom of those who have had to deal with quite variable scenarios—we present some choices.

If the individual with a mood disorder and the organisation in which they work can negotiate a humane and practical balance both will benefit, bringing Winston Churchill's maxim to mind: 'We make a living by what we get, but we make a life by what we give.'

Appendix 1
Work Wellbeing Questionnaire

This is a measure available on the Black Dog Institute website (see www.blackdoginstitute.org.au/surveys/workwellbeing/index.cfm) which assesses facets of employee satisfaction in the workplace. It can provide you with a comparative profile of your work environment in terms of the extent to which it advances your sense of wellbeing or not.

Notes

Introduction

1   M. Johnstone and A. Johnstone, *Living with a Black Dog: How to take care of someone with depression while looking after yourself*, Pan Macmillan, Sydney, 2008.

Chapter 1

1   C.J.L. Murray and A.D. Lopez AD (eds), *Global Burden of Disease: A comprehensive assessment of mortality and disability from diseases, injuries, and risk factors in 1990 and projected to 2020*, Harvard School of Public Health, Cambridge, MA, 1999.

2   A. Kielhorn, J.M. Graf von der Schulenberg, *The Health Economics Handbook* (2nd edn), Chester: Adis International, 2000.

3   T. Slade, A. Johnston, M. Teeson, H. Whiteford, P. Burgess, J. Pirkis and S. Saw, *The Mental Health of Australians 2; Report on the 2007 National Survey of Mental Health and Wellbeing*, Department of Health and Ageing, Canberra, 2009.

4   R.C. Kessler, W.T. Chiu, O. Demler and E.E. Walters, 'Prevalence, severity, and comorbidity of twelve-month DSM-IV disorders in the National Comorbidity Survey Replication (NCS-R)', *Archives of General Psychiatry*, 2005, 62(6): 617–27.

5   *National Survey of Mental Health and Wellbeing of Australians: Summary of results*, Australian Bureau of Statistics (ABS), Canberra, 2008.

6   B.F. Grant, F.S. Stinson, D.S. Hasin, D.A. Dawson, W.J. Ruan and B.Z. Huang, 'Prevalence, correlates and comorbidity of DSM-IV Bipolar I Disorder and Axis I and II Disorders: Results from the National Epidemiologic Survey on Alcohol and Related Conditions', *Journal of Clinical Psychiatry*, 2005, 66: 1205–15.

7   *Mental Health at Work: Developing the business case*, Policy Paper 8, 2006/07, The
    Sainsbury Centre for Mental Health, London.

8   *Mental Health at Work: From defining to solving the problem*, Chair in Corporate
    Occupational Health and Safety Management, Université Laval, Quebec, Canada, 2003.

9   R.C. Kessler, P. Berglund, O. Demler, R. Jin, K.R. Merikangas and E.E. Walters,
    'Lifetime prevalence and age-of-onset distributions of DSM-IV disorders in the
    National Comorbidity Survey Replication', *Archives of General Psychiatry*, 2005,
    62: 593–602.

10 The Queensland Centre for Mental Health: www.qcsr.uq.edu.au and www.qcmhr.uq.edu.
    au/worc.

11 M. Ellison, Z. Russinova, J. Massaro and A. Lyass, 'People with schizophrenia employed
    as professionals and managers: Initial evidence and exploration', *Schizophrenia Research*,
    2005, 76(2): 123–5.

12 *Mental Health: A Report of the Surgeon General*, US Department of Health and Human
    Services, Substance Abuse and Mental Health Services Administration, Center for Mental
    Health Services, National Institutes of Health, National Institute of Mental Health,
    Rockville, MD, 1999.

13 beyondblue, The National Depression Initiative, Australia: www.beyondblue.org.au.

14 *The Healthy Thinking Initiative*, Workplace and Mental Health Statistics compiled by the
    American Psychological Association, quoted from the National Committee for Quality
    Assurance, 2004.

15 *Mental Health at Work: Developing the business case*, op. cit.

16 J. Calabrese, University of Cleveland, quoted in 'Workplaces quit quietly ignoring mental
    illness', by S. Armour, *USA Today*, 22 August 2006.

17 T. Slade et al., op. cit.

18 L. Elinson, P. Houck, S.C. Marcus and H.A. Pincus, 'Depression and the ability to work',
    Psychiatric Services, 2004, 55: 29–34.

19 W.F. Stewart, J.A. Ricci, E. Chee, S.R. Hahn and D. Morganstein, 'Cost of lost productive
    work time among US workers with depression', *The Journal of the American Medical
    Association*, 2003, 289(3): 3135–44.

20 R.C. Kessler, H.S. Akiskal, M. Ames, H. Birnbaum, P. Greenberg, R.M. Hirschfeld, R. Jin,
    K.R. Merikangas, G.E. Simon and P.S. Wang, 'Prevalence and effects of mood disorders

on work performance in a nationally representative sample of US workers', *American Journal of Psychiatry*, 2006, 163: 1561–8.

21 *Mental Health at Work: Developing the business case*, op. cit.

22 M. Wilson, R. Joffe and B. Wilkerson, 'The unheralded business crisis in Canada: Depression at work', Global Business and Economic Roundtable on Addiction and Mental Health, Toronto, 2002.

Chapter 2

1   M.G. Patterson, M.A. West, R. Lawthom and S. Nickell, *The Sheffield Effectiveness Program. Issues in People Management: Impact of people management practices on business performance*, Institute of Work Psychology, University of Sheffield and Centre for Economic Performance, London School of Economics, 2008.

2   A.D. LaMontagne, McCaughey Centre, VicHealth Centre for the Promotion of Mental Health and Community Wellbeing, University of Melbourne with Monash University and British Columbia University, *BMC Public Health*: www.emaxhealth.com/25/22721. html, 2008.

3   Office of Communications and Public Liaison, NIMH, Information Resources and Inquiries Branch: www.healthieryou.com/depworker.html.

4   P.S. Wang, G.E. Simon, J. Avorn, F. Azocar, E.J. Ludman, J. McCulloch, M.Z. Petukhova and R.C. Kessler, 'Telephone screening, outreach and care management for depressed workers and impact on clinical and work productivity outcomes: A randomized controlled trial', *Journal of the American Medical Association*, 2007, 298(12): 1401–11.

5   C. Tennant, 'Work-related stress and depressive disorders', *Journal of Psychosomatic Research*, 2001, 51(5): 697–704.

6   A.D. LaMontagne, T. Keegel, D. Vallance, A. Ostry and R. Wolfe, 'Job strain-attributable depression in a sample of working Australians: Assessing the contribution to health inequalities', *BMC Public Health*, 2008, 8(181). At www.biomedcentral.com/content/ pdf/1471-2458-8-181.pdf.

7   M.F. Hilton, P.A. Scuffham, J.D. Sheridan, C.M. Cleary, N. Vecchio and H.A. Whiteford, 'The association between mental disorders and productivity in treated and untreated employees', *Journal of Occupational and Environmental Medicine*, 2009, 51(9): 996–1003.

8   The American Institute of Stress, Yonkers, NY.

9   C. Tennant, op. cit.

10   A.D. LaMontagne et al., op. cit.

Chapter 3

1   N. Highett, beyondblue, The National Depression Initiative: www.beyondblue.org.au.

2   From *Depression in the Workplace*, Information booklet, Royal College of Psychiatrists, UK, 1999: www.rcpsych.ac.uk/pdf/Depressionworkplace.pdf.

3   R.C. Kessler, H.S. Akiskal, M. Ames, H. Birnbaum, P. Greenberg, R.M. Hirschfeld, R. Jin, K.R. Merikangas, G.E. Simon and P.S. Wang, 'Prevalence and effects of mood disorders on work performance in a nationally representative sample of US workers', *American Journal of Psychiatry*, 2006, 163: 1561–8.

4   *Bipolar Disorder*, Education Booklet, National Institute of Mental Health (NIMH), Bethesda, MD 20892-9663, 2009: www.nimh.nih.gov/health/publications/bipolar-disorder/index.shtml.

Chapter 4

1   A. Baxter, H.A. Whiteford, C.M. Cleary and M.F. Hilton, 'Association between treatment-seeking behaviour for mental health and employment status in a national study', *Australian and New Zealand Journal of Psychiatry*, 2007, 41(S. 1), 4:A2–A101.

2   B. McNair, Mental Health @ Work: www.mhatwork.com.au.

3   'Team Resilience Program', information from A. Kuhnen MD, MPH, Vice President, Employee Health Management US, GlaxoSmithKline, Philadelphia, PA, to C. Mamberto, *The Wall Street Journal*, 13 August 2007.

4   D.A. Adler, T.J. McLaughlin, W.H. Rogers, H. Chang, L. Lapitsky and D. Lerner, 'Job performance deficits due to depression', *American Journal of Psychiatry*, 2006, 163: 1569–76.

5   P.J. Sadler, 'Leadership style, confidence in management, and job satisfaction', *Journal of Applied Behavioural Science*, 1970, 6: 3–19.

Chapter 5

1   J. Arehart-Treichel, 'Universal coverage doesn't ensure people will seek treatment', *Psychiatric News*, 21 October 2005, 40(20): 27, American Psychiatric Association: www.cpa-apc.org/Publications/CJP/current/cjp-sept-05-vasiliadis-7.pdf.

2   The Queensland Centre for Mental Health: www.qcsr.uq.edu.au and www.qcmhr.uq.edu. au/worc.

Chapter 6

1   From *Depression in the Workplace*, Information booklet, Royal College of Psychiatrists, UK, 1999: www.rcpsych.ac.uk/pdf/Depressionworkplace.pdf.

2   'Returning to work: The role of depression', study by Loughborough University (Mental Health Foundation Grant), UK, February 2009: www.mentalhealth.org.uk/return-to-work.

Chapter 7

1   D.A. Dunstan, 'Are sickness certificates doing our patients harm?', *Australian Family Physician*, 2009, 38(1/2): 61–3.

2   From *Depression in the Workplace*, Information booklet, Royal College of Psychiatrists, UK, 1999: www.rcpsych.ac.uk/pdf/Depressionworkplace.pdf.

3   'Husky Injection Moulding Systems', Organizational Profiles; Human Resources and Skills Development Canada: www.hrsdc.gc.ca/eng/lp/spila/wlb/ell/08husky_injection_ moulding_systems.shtml (accessed 8 July, 2010).

4   J.G. Proudfoot, P.J. Corr, D.E. Guest and G. Dunn, 'Cognitive-behavioural training to change attributional style improves employee wellbeing, job satisfaction, productivity and turnover', *Personality and Individual Differences*, 2009, 46: 147–53.

Chapter 8

1   A. Mungovan and F. Quigley, *Choosing Your Path: Disclosure, it's a personal issue*, Regional Disability Liaison Team, Greater Western Sydney Region and Western Victoria Region, Australia, 2004: http://pubsites.uws.edu.au/rdlo/disclosure/pdfs/ disclosure.pdf.

Chapter 9

1   *Living well with a psychiatric disability in work and school*, Center for Psychiatric Rehabilitation, Boston University, 2007: www.bu.edu/cpr/jobschool.

2   A. Young, 'What do workers want most?', Utah State University Extension, 2001: http:// extension.usu.edu/dairy/files/uploads/htms/workers.htm.

3   R.J. Paul, 'Managing employee depression in the workplace', *Review of Business*, Winter, 2003: www.entrepreneur.com/tradejournals/article/97892563_4.html.

4   P. Hall-Jones, 'What makes a good job?', *Public Services International*, 2006: www. world-psi.org/Template.cfm?Section=Home&CONTENTID=10816&TEMPLATE=/ ContentManagement/ContentDisplay.cfm.

5   R.J. Paul, op. cit.

6   R.J. Paul, op. cit.

Chapter 10

1   A. Horin, 'Here's a stimulating idea: Create jobs', *Sydney Morning Herald*, 14–15 February 2009.

Chapter 11

1   Some ideas adapted from the Department of Education, Employment and Workplace Relations (DEEWR): *Family-friendly work arrangements*, 2009: www.deewr.gov.au/ freshideas.

2   *Mental Health at Work: From defining to solving the problem*, Chair in Corporate Occupational Health and Safety Management, Université Laval, Quebec, Canada, 2003.

Index